Conservation in Action:

Chester's Bridgegate

Donald W. Insall
OBE, FSA, FRIBA, FRTPI, SP Dip(Hons)
Conservation Consultant to the City of Chester

and
Department of the Environment
Directorate of Ancient Monuments and Historic Buildings

London: Her Majesty's Stationery Office

© Crown copyright 1982
First published 1982

Printed in England for Her Majesty's Stationery Office
by Hobbs the Printers of Southampton
(1737) Dd0717306 C20 9/82 G381

Design by HMSO Graphic Design

ISBN 0 11 751554 X

Foreword

by the Secretary of State for the Environment

Conservation in an historic town centre

In 1968, my predecessor was pleased to give his support to detailed studies of four of our historic towns — Bath, Chester, Chichester and York. They provided a springboard for conservation policy and initiative throughout the country. The Chester Study was undertaken by Donald W Insall and Associates. It recommended an active conservation programme to save the character and vitality of the City, and has provided the basis for the City's energetic conservation activities over the past decade.

Nowhere was action more urgently required than in a very decayed part of the walled city called Bridgegate. In bringing this area back to life we have learned much and the message of this report is that, by a mixture of direct action and continuous encouragement, areas which are economically and physically in decay can be revived and their historic character secured for future generations.

The skills used to tackle Bridgegate's problems offer valuable guidelines for urban conservation. I therefore commend this report to all who care about the future of our historic towns.

Plate 3a The Secretary of State on his tour of Chester in 1980

Plate 4a An early print of Gamul House. Compare this with the illustration on p.38

Contents

[To enable financial sums expended at different times to be compared directly, they are related whenever possible to their 1979 equivalent. These equivalent values are set in italics and, where they occur within the body of the text, they are enclosed in square brackets.]

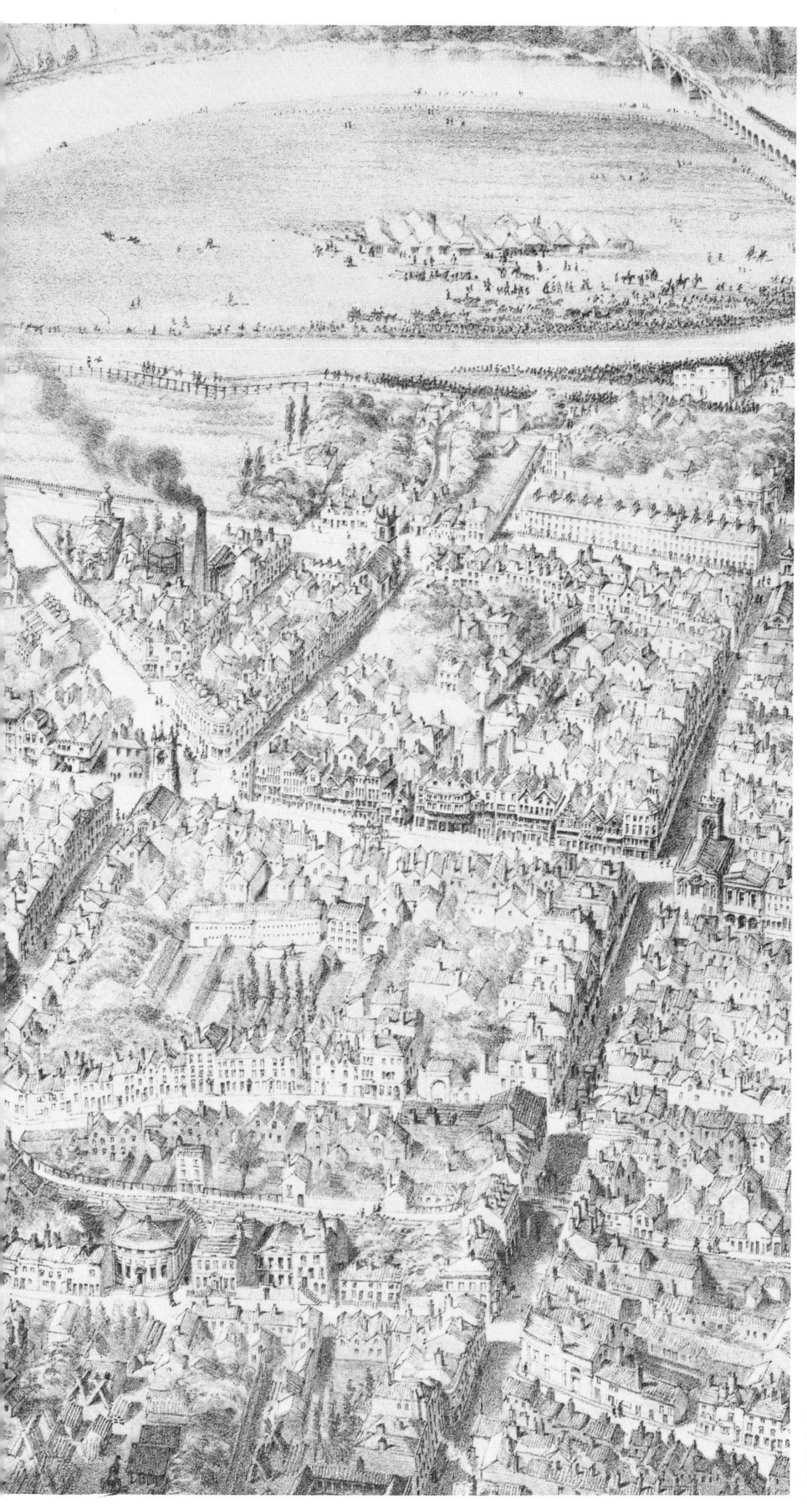

Plate 6a Part of
Chester *circa* 1855,
from a panoramic
study signed by John
McGahey

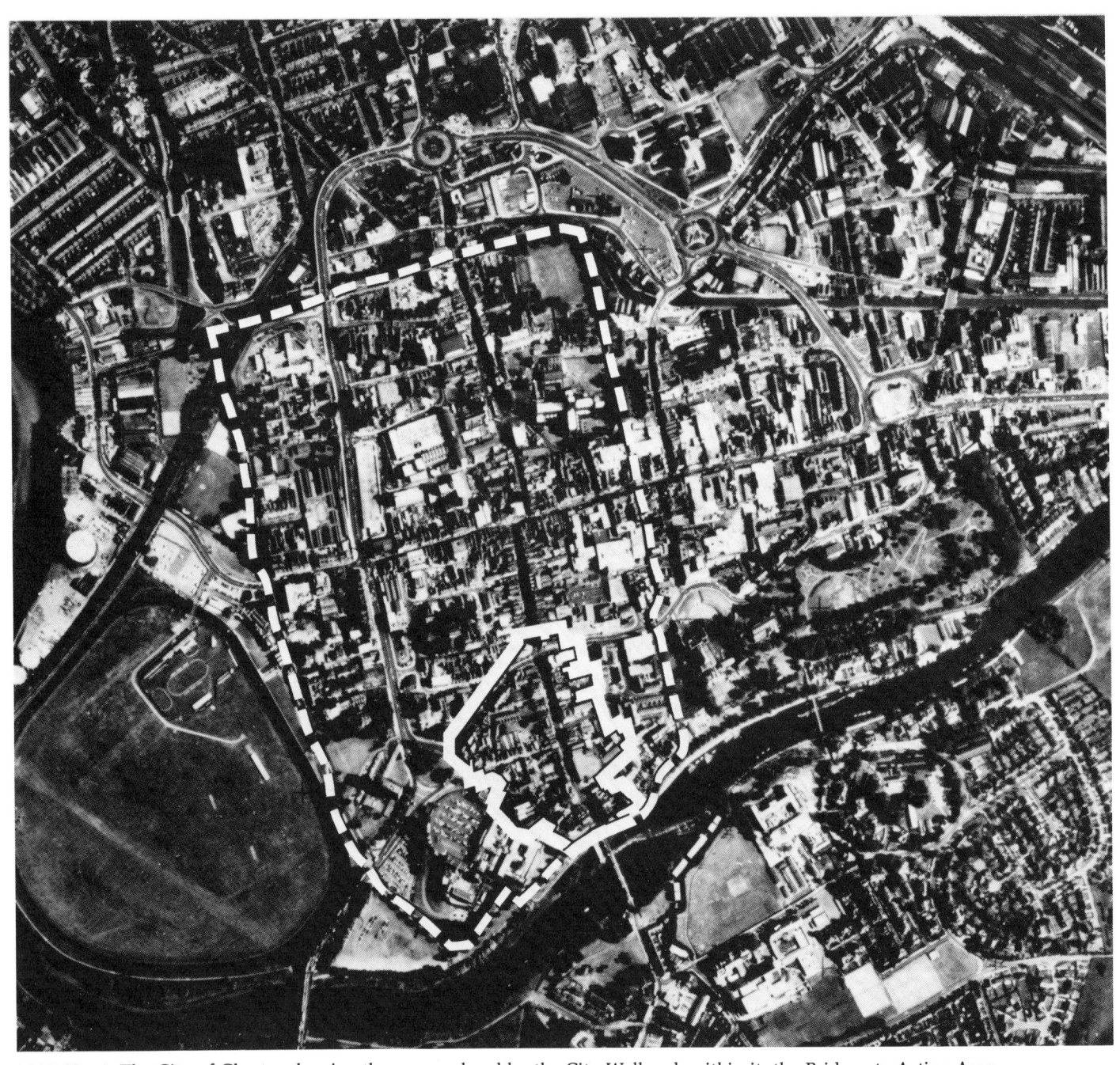

MAP No. 1 The City of Chester showing the area enclosed by the City Wall and, within it, the Bridgegate Action Area.

1 The four study towns

1.1 National pilot studies

The last two decades have marked an increased public awareness and concern at the apparently headlong destruction and decay of our historic towns. Faced with the damaging pressures of modern transport, of commercial demand and of accelerating architectural change, they have been seriously threatened. The need for concerted action at local and national levels led to the commissioning of four pilot 'Conservation Studies'. One of these, commissioned jointly by the City Council and the Ministry of Housing and Local Government, was devoted to the historic City of Chester. Donald W Insall and Associates were appointed in 1966 to undertake this study of the character of the city, its opportunities and problems and to recommend solutions not only to Chester but to other historic towns. Similar studies by other consultants were undertaken in York, Bath and Chichester.

1.2 'Chester – a study in conservation' 1968

The historic centre of Chester, consisting of the walled City with its immediate surroundings, is for the most part a thriving one. It is also extremely attractive, possessing a great wealth of old and beautiful buildings. The Chester Study first undertook a detailed survey of the existing historic fabric in relation to its geographical region, its urban setting and its people. Regional economic pressures and changing trade and transport patterns were analysed in relation to their effect on the walled City. Land use pressures and property demand within the city were studied; problem and opportunity areas were identified and examined in depth; townscape elements and qualities were assessed; initial surveys were made to define the historic importance, ownership, condition and use-potential of over 400 key buildings; finally the consultants analysed the three elements which contribute so much to the city's character – the 'Rows', the City Walls and its Riverside.

The Study stressed the importance of human attachment of people to their place – a vital but unquantifiable force in the life of a city. It also stressed a point often forgotten, namely that the main source of money for conserving buildings arises from their own value: an essential dimension of every building is its repair and maintenance cost in relation to its market value over and above that of its site.

The art of managing a Conservation Action Programme in a city like Chester is, in large measure, simply that of matching likely cost with available return. To do this effectively means:
1. recognising latent property values,
2. using every available resource including grant-aid, and
3. intervening in just sufficient measure to save each building that contributes to the quality of life in the town.

The Study pointed out that the compound effect of one property upon another in a run-down area is profound and sensitive. A Conservation Programme must identify problems and opportunities, and act as something of a marriage-broker between the two. To achieve a long-term recovery of property values often demands a short-term injection of money. This need has to be recognised and accepted.

The analysis introduced the principle of 'Capacity Planning', balancing the appetites of an area with its capacity for accommodating change. It examined the traffic and pedestrian circulation pattern, and proposed improvements designed to ease and restrain pressures within the natural capacity of the city centre. Proposals were made to improve the integrated use of public and private transport. A new and more central bus station was planned, together with more localised car parking, to be followed by a gradually developing programme of traffic management, all with their emphasis upon the comfort of the shopping pedestrian. The same approach was later applied to the capacity of the urban fabric to absorb major shopping and office space demands which since the early 'seventies had begun to pose a threat to the city's character.

1.2.1 Study Areas and Conservation Action Sites

Selected Study Areas were surveyed in depth, appraising in detail their townscape quality and the merits of individual buildings, together with their ownership, condition and use-potential. Within these areas, 'Conservation Action Sites' were defined, redevelopment opportunities were outlined and potential environmental improvements were proposed.

1.2.2 Legislation

A special legal section of the report was submitted early in 1967 when new Listed Building legislation was in preparation. It contained detailed suggestions for improvements in the everyday efficiency of control and planning procedures.

1.2.3 A Conservation Action Programme

The report broke new ground in preparing a phased and costed programme of action. This comprised environmental improvements, pilot redevelopment schemes, 'first-aid' protection, building repairs and combined conversion/repair schemes. Building works were costed and arranged within an initial five-year and a subsequent ten-year programme.

The programme identified 28 buildings in need of 'first-aid' (including 12 in Bridgegate), 142 in need of action within the first five years (33 in Bridgegate), and 229 other buildings requiring action in the second phase (35 in Bridgegate). The cost of the initial five-year programme was estimated at £900,000 [£5,022,000]* (£360,000 [£2,008,800]* in Bridgegate). (Table 1 on page 21 shows expenditure of £1,446,360 in Bridgegate over the eight-year period 1972 to 1979 at 1979 prices.)

Chester is now one of a number of major towns with

---

*1979 equivalent amounts indicated throughout the study in square brackets, thus: [ ].

similar rolling programmes of conservation activity, aided by DOE allocations and spread over a period of three years or more. The 1968 Report on the city therefore set the pattern for more effective town conservation both locally and nationally by advocating costed programmes of grant-aided conservation activity.

1.3 National action

The four reports were considered by the Preservation Policy Group, a government-appointed committee under the chairmanship of Lord Kennet, who was the Minister primarily concerned with conservation at the time. The Group recommended that subsidies should be given to enable local authorities to undertake new 'General Conservation Schemes' and that Pilot Schemes be set up immediately in each of the four pilot towns. They pressed for increased powers for local authorities, both for historic buildings in their own care and those in private ownership. They also recommended the production of technical reports on aspects of conservation.

Most of the recommendations were subsequently adopted. In place of the 'General Conservation Scheme' subsidy, a new flexible conservation grant was introduced in 1972 under Section 10 of the Town and Country Planning (Amendment) Act. Over five hundred towns have since benefited from S10 grants. Grant aid under combined DOE/Local Authority arrangements known as 'Town Schemes' has also increased steadily; and the number of Town Schemes rose from 12 in 1970 to 131 in 1979.

Pilot schemes were selected in York, Bath and Chester. The early Bath scheme was on a small scale and was rapidly completed (Old Orchard Street/Pierrepont Place). That in York was centred on the run-down Aldwark quarter, the aim being to reintroduce residencial use in place of industry and warehousing, whilst keeping the old buildings that remained and encouraging upper floor uses in the perimeter shopping streets. Like the Chester Pilot Scheme in Bridgegate, the Aldwark project is long-term; but there is ample evidence of steady progress towards the goal originally set out in the York Conservation Study. Bridgegate was selected as Chester's pilot scheme in 1971. Of all the areas within the walled city, it provided by far the greatest challenge. The 1968 Chester Conservation Study made this very plain.

This report is an attempt to show the progress made during the 'seventies and to indicate the problems which remain to be solved. But over and above these are the pioneering organisational and financial measures adopted in Chester, which the present report will discuss in detail. These, even more than the actual work on the ground, can be an inspiration and guide to other historic towns.

2 Chester

2.1 The commitment to conservation

By defining the shape and scope for conservation activity in the City and giving a clear indication of the necessary scale of financial commitment, the Chester Conservation Study alerted both the local authority and central government to the opportunity for effective action. A sustained public concern, supported by and reflected in the local and national press, created a strong political climate for urban conservation. The report *Chester: A Study in Conservation* was published by HMSO in 1968 and was formally accepted by resolution of the City Council in 1969.

2.2 Grant aid

2.2.1 *The Conservation Fund*

Directly following publication of the Conservation Study, the City Council made the decision to commit the City fully to an active Conservation Programme. The main springboard was the pioneering decision to levy a special Conservation Rate. Each year the product of a 2d rate (then £29,000 [£116,000]) was put into a Conservation Fund which was so organised that it could be carried over from one financial year to the next. This was particularly valuable in the early 1970s when many schemes were waiting to get off the ground and money would otherwise have been lost by default.

At first, requests for grant-aid were few, making it possible to reserve money in anticipation of the high outlay required when the Conservation Programme began to take effect. The rate level was soon increased to one new penny (£36,000) and then in 1973-74 to 1½p (£55,000 [£111,640]). But by 1974 even this was found to be insufficient to cope with the scale of activity, and the rate was increased during the next two years to bring in £100,000 [£175,000] per annum. However, because of the general economic situation the Fund was cut back to £80,000 [£132,800] in 1976-77 and the following year it was further reduced to just over £50,000 [74,000]. It remained at £50,000 [£65,000] in 1978-79 and rose to £90,000 again in 1979-80. The details are set out in Graph Nos 1 and 2.

The Fund has been used for both the repair and improvement of properties and has been combined with Historic Building Grants from the DOE.

2.2.2 *Town Scheme Grants (DOE Contribution)*

Most of the money from the Fund was allocated to the 'Town Scheme' where it was matched by central government money. The annual DOE allocation for 1970-71, the first year, was a modest £10,000 [£40,000] increasing to £25,000 [£72,000] in 1972–73. But from 1973–74 to 1975–76 the Department allocated £100,000 [£184,000] per annum to the Chester Town Scheme. In 1976-77 it was agreed that the Department's allocation could be increased to £115,000 [£190,000] so that the impact of conservation work could be maintained whilst the City Council conservation budget suffered from the current economic cutbacks. In the event the amount needed from the DOE was £83,220 [£138,700]. The scheme was then renewed for three years (April 1977 to April 1980) but, as a result of the council's continuing financial difficulties, at the reduced level for that period of £75,000 [£111,000] per annum from DOE. By 1975 some £200,000 of public funds was being attracted to the area so that, despite the cutback in grant-aid in the late 1970s, the 'flywheel' effect of momentum gained up to 1976 enabled much progress to be made during the second half of the decade.

2.2.3 *Conservation Area Grants*

Chester was also able to benefit from the financial assistance available from the government under Section 10 of the 1972 Town and Country Planning (Amendment) Act for the enhancement of 'outstanding' conservation areas. The salary of a full-time conservation officer was partially met from this source of Government money and a 50 per cent contribution has been made towards the Insall consultancy. In 1979-80 about £78,000 was contributed under Section 10.

2.2.4 *Combining grants*

Under the Town Scheme the contribution is usually divided evenly between the local authority and central government and amounts to half the total cost of repair work. However, if the local authority owns the property, it will have to find three-quarters of the cost. It was to encourage Chester City Council to purchase endangered buildings that the DOE agreed to contribute 50 per cent of the total cost of their repair following acquisition by the City. In addition, a 'one-off' allocation of £50,000 [£87,500] was made by the DOE in 1974 to help the City to acquire key properties.

To increase the viability of a restoration scheme, the owner sometimes needs more than one type of grant. He should also consider applying for aid from other sources, such as house improvement grants.

2.2.5 *Future levels of grant*

The City Council intend to allocate the product of 1p rate – £200,000 per annum – to the fund from April 1980 for three years whilst the DOE have agreed to allocate £130,000 towards the Town Scheme rising to £150,000 in 1982-83. In addition, £80,000 was reserved under Section 10 in 1980-81. These increases will help to offset the effects of inflation and VAT.

2.3 The conservation team

The political commitment and financial provision were complemented by setting up a conservation team. In the main this comprised the Conservation Section within the Planning Department and the conservation consultants, Donald W Insall and Associates, who were commissioned to help implement the programme outlined in their 1968 study.

The team had to be of sufficient stature to command ready support, and since the senior officers of a local authority each have many commitments in other directions, it had to be able to promote delegated action in a spirit of mutual trust. The DOE has kept a watching brief at all stages, and has given valuable advice and practical encouragement. This teamwork has in turn relied upon the energetic readiness of local contractors and craftsmen to undertake the difficult and sometimes daunting task of renewing old and complicated structures.

The following paragraphs set out the main elements of the conservation team in Chester.

2.3.1 The Planning Committee and the Council's Officers

In Chester, the Development and Planning Committee, and in particular its successive chairmen, have played a key role in the Conservation Programme. This Programme was started by the former County Borough Council and, because of staff continuity, was uninterrupted by Local Government reorganisation.

2.3.2 Chester City: Conservation Section

The prime responsibility for Conservation has been exercised by the Planning Department of the Council, first as a Division of the City Engineer's Department of the former Borough Council, and following reorganisation, as a Division of the Directorate of Technical Services.

In 1971, it was recommended that a closer link be forged between the Town Hall and local residents, and the new post of conservation officer was created. This was the first such appointment in Britain, and has proved one of the most significant steps in establishing essential rapport with property owners and local people.

On the recommendation of the consultants, and with DOE financial support, the council has now been able to build up an effective Conservation Section within its Planning Department to cope with the increasing momentum of work. The conservation officer's 'approachability' and the enthusiasm of the Section have been key factors in establishing a good relationship between the owners of buildings needing help and the source of that help. The Section operates in association with the conservation consultants, and now consists of the conservation officer and two conservation assistants.

2.3.3 Conservation consultants

The task of the consultants has been to promote the City's programme, with a special responsibility for the Bridgegate Action Area. This has made available the resources of specialists in architectural, structural and quantity surveying work on historic buildings. A nationally based consultant demonstrably has no local axe to grind and can view local influences objectively. The continuity of the same consultants has provided ten years experience of the particular problems in Chester, and this continuity has proved invaluable; they have played a vital role in promoting conservation progress.

2.3.4 Department of the Environment

The Chester Programme has derived consistent support from the DOE and the Historic Buildings Council for England. The Department sets aside an annual sum to ensure that steady progress is maintained*.

2.3.5 The public

Throughout the Programme, local people have shown intense interest and have given valuable support to conservation. This is best demonstrated by their ready commitment to the City Conservation Fund, which has never been a controversial topic in Chester.

Consistently helpful and responsible comment and publicity have been given by the local press, who have kept in touch with the progress of the work, and have published many special articles on the major projects undertaken. One local newspaper even donated the public clock which now graces the tower of St Michael's Church, Chester's new Heritage Centre.

Building owners and occupiers have been kept closely in touch with the Conservation Action Programme, for example by Bulletins distributed in the Action Area and by meetings of people affected by proposals in any locality. In some instances, the City has directly commissioned surveys and reports upon which action can then be taken by private owners. Local surveyors and land and estate agents have been closely concerned in negotiating each detailed project.

2.3.6 The professions

Without committed public support, neither the elected representatives nor local authority officers could carry through a conservation programme on anything like the scale now established in Chester. The Conservation Area Advisory Committee, set up in 1970, has given continuous advice to the Development and Planning Committee on developments affecting Chester's conservation area. The Chester Civic Trust contributed generously towards the cost of reinstating Chester's High Cross. The Cheshire Society of Architects has held conservation lectures and contributed publicity during Architectural Heritage Year, and its members have been individually involved in many conservation projects.

2.3.7 Contractors and craftsmen

During the course of the Action Programme, with increasing experience, local firms have often shown themselves to be capable of responding to conservation needs. Their selection has been based on their previous performance and expertise rather than through general advertisements. This could with advantage be based on the type of contract record form reproduced in Appendix A. Standards of craftmanship have varied, and the pointing of brickwork especially seems to call for better training. Local craftsmanship in timber has however, demonstrated a high standard; and so has the capacity of contractors to adapt themselves to the exacting and often unforeseeable demands of older structures.

2.3.8 Suppliers of building materials

One essential need on conservation work is a stock of suitable materials. Sometimes the same products are still

---

*A film recording progress in Chester and the lessons to be learned was produced by the Department in 1976. This film – *The Conservation Game* – is available in both English and French from the DOE Film Library, and has been widely shown.

being made; but just as often they are now available only as expensive 'specials' such as moulded cast-iron rainwater heads or decorative iron brackets. At other times, the product is no longer available, eg 'ton' slates or local clay wall-copings. Even when a version of the same item is still available for repairs, the crispness of the new material may too easily look out of place in an old building whose other elements have gently softened with age. Despite the cost of suitable space, a store of second-hand materials is therefore a most valuable asset. Chester City Council have now established a 'materials bank' under the control of the Conservation Section, the results of which have already been put to good use in current projects.

When consent is granted to demolish a building in the conservation area, a condition is imposed requiring the owner to allow the City to prepare a schedule of materials suitable for salvage and re-use and to negotiate a purchase price. The chairman of the Development and Planning Committee has authority to approve any purchase of potentially useful materials from the Conservation Fund of up to £250. Demolition contractors have been particularly co-operative in this arrangement.

Plate 13a Chester's Bridgegate: St Mary's Hill

3 The Bridgegate Action Area

3.1 Character

The Bridgegate Area was a particularly run-down quarter within the walled City. It is located at the north end of the Old Dee Bridge – the original river crossing point. From here it runs up the south-facing sandstone slope towards the city centre but stopping short of the lively shopping-area centred on the famous Rows. The area defined for action is shown on Map No. 1.

The spine of Bridgegate is Lower Bridge Street, the old route northwards from the Bridge to the Cross. Two small streets (St. Olave's Street and Duke Street) run off to the east and the western part of the area centres about Castle Street. Down its west perimeter between Bridgegate and the Castle the old packhorse route of St. Mary's Hill descends precipitously to the former Shipgate, once a thriving element in Chester's medieval port. But the port is no more and the whole Bridgegate quarter was cut off in the nineteenth century by a new road, Grosvenor Street, which cut a diagonal route across the city's otherwise consistent gridiron plan.

Within Bridgegate, the street pattern, trees, cobbled ways and contrasting buildings of differing periods and quality serve to produce a varied townscape of great interest. The buildings date predominantly from the seventeenth and eighteenth centuries, but many contain remnants of much earlier structures, some of which may have been damaged when the city was under seige during the Civil War, or by the numerous fires in the seventeenth century.

Lower Bridge Street formed the main route to the City centre from the higher port and the Dee Mills. Some of its buildings now have shops at ground level, with characteristic high-arched openings over the steps leading up to the living accommodation at first floor level. These used to give access via a passage to small cottages on the backland; but these back cottages, with their minimal floor areas, were nearly all demolished some years ago, a rare survival being Gamul Place.

The famous Rows which form such a predominant feature of the city's central area, and which are such a riddle for historians, once extended down Lower Bridge Street. A number of significant medieval buildings, such as The Falcon, the Old King's Head and Tudor House, retain evidence of earlier Rows which have been enclosed under licence to form the front rooms of the houses. Only one building, No. 11 Lower Bridge Street, still has an exposed Row.

Apart from a small amount of warehousing and light industry and the numerous public houses and shops on Lower Bridge Street, the area has a residential tradition. Large town houses, such as 15 and 17 Castle Street, Gamul House and the Oddfellows' Hall were built here by wealthy landowners, but most of these were subsequently sub-divided into tenements or used for other purposes. The Falcon was at one time a town house of the Grosvenors, and the Bear and Billet was built as a town house by the Earl of Shrewsbury.

3.2 Problems

Because the Bridgegate area remained comparatively unsuccessful, its buildings have not been altered and thus retain much of major historic value, albeit often in a desperately declining condition. Of Lower Bridge Street the 1968 Report observed: 'the street's main characteristic is unfortunately the visual poverty resulting from its fundamental problem, the disuse and decay of many of its fine buildings. This is one of Chester's worst examples of area decline, and a solution is urgent'.

The choice of Bridgegate as the Action Area was therefore both purposeful and courageous. The sector had suffered for many years from economic decline and steady physical decay. Clearly if such an area could be resus-

Plates 14a and 15a Parts of the east side of Lower Bridge Street in about 1820. St Olave's Church is on the left

citated without losing any of its historic identity the case for urban conservation would be proven. Moreover the lessons learned would be of enormous interest to other towns and even other countries, not least because renewal would be achieved within the normal roles of the public and private sectors: there would be no wholesale 'takeover' by the government, local authority, private company or any other body; no major new economic force would come on the scene to rescue the declining area.

This is not to say there were to be no new initiatives. The organisation within the City Council, local authority and central government support, and the continued employment of the consultants have all played an essential role in concentrating energy and effort over a prolonged period on a problem not susceptible by British standards to any single or simple solution.

The problem is not solely one of decline and decay. Within the area were found an extraordinary mixture of properties of all sizes and ages, many of which were individually and structurally complex. This was matched by the variety of uses – residential, commercial, industrial, office, educational and open space. Ageing residents, redundant buildings, blighted areas, out-of-scale redevelopment and parked cars all added to the range of difficulties, whilst the road system isolated this quarter of the town from the main centre of urban activity. This isolation invested Bridgegate with a traditional and almost Dickensian character where time had stood still whilst the bulk of the properties quietly and steadily deteriorated – in some instances to the verge of collapse.

By 1971 some key steps had been taken – mainly of a financial and organisational nature – but the neglect and decline had become even more evident. Much of Bridgegate was a depressed area, visually blighted by misused, empty and near-derelict buildings. The situation was breeding insecurity and pessimism among the remaining inhabitants. The ills of the area were spreading like an epidemic; intensive care, financial assistance and careful attention were becoming daily more necessary.

3.3 Bridgegate Action Programme: Interim Report No. 1*

In 1971 the City Council therefore directed its Planning Department, in association with Donald W. Insall and Associates, to carry out a much more detailed survey of the Bridgegate area, and to recommend ways of promoting a conservation policy by identifying properties whose future security most depended on immediate action by the public sector.

3.3.1 Aims

The prime aim of the Report was to gather such information as was needed to gain greater understanding of causes and effects. No small detail could be overlooked or discarded. Each piece would sooner or later fill its own gap in the conservation jig-saw. In studying individual buildings, the team evaluated their relative historic and architectural value, their condition and layout, amenities and environment. Above all they took account of the relationship between each building and its owner and occupants, whose circumstances, needs and ambitions proved to be of key significance.

But the gathering of information was not the only aim of the first report on Bridgegate. The most important findings led immediately to specific recommendations for emergency action. Some properties of critical importance needed immediate attention, and it was increasingly necessary for the City to give a lead. The 1971 Report therefore recommended that certain key properties be acquired by the local authority without delay.

3.3.2 Methods

The newly appointed conservation officer had accumulated useful data, and the evident improvement in public relations was of immediate help in establishing an understanding with local people. Experience had already shown the importance of public involvement and information from the earliest stage, to avoid generating any feeling of apprehension and insecurity among the inhabitants of such a vulnerable area. In Bridgegate, all the owners and occupiers of the buildings were first sent an explanatory letter and appointments were then made for a member of the survey team to visit each building. A temporary office base was set up in Lower Bridge Street and maximum press publicity was encouraged. The detailed survey was carried out

*Bridgegate Action Programme. Interim Report No. 1 Donald W. Insall & Associates, 1971.

basically in two weeks by a team of five architects and planners. All survey information was collected upon specifically designed standard forms to ensure parity and to assist subsequent collation. It was directed to the following main aspects:

1. ownership, tenancy and use,
2. building/user relationship,
3. fitness for use,
4. condition,
5. finances required and possible resources,
6. incentives for beneficial change, if required, and
7. external pressures.

The overriding aim was to assess not only the physical state of each building, but also how to secure its long-term social and economic viability.

In December 1971 the consultants submitted the report to the City Council and the DOE, setting out their findings.

3.3.3. *Findings*

The evidence of decline was clear. Seventy-seven buildings were inspected, many of which were unoccupied. Of this total, 49 were found to be in need of substantial repair and/or improvement. Most significantly, of the occupied buildings, 16 were found to be 'at risk' due simply to inertia on the part of their owners who, discouraged about their neighbourhood and its uncertain future, considered their property to be virtually blighted. The most common physical problems and their causes were identified as follows:

1. Defective roofs, gutters and upper walls – due mainly to access difficulties and to uncertainties about responsibilities at party divisions.
2. Disuse at upper floor levels – caused by imbalance between building sizes and the needs of occupants.
3. Dereliction of rear additions – arising from their mainly poor construction and from maintenance problems.
4. Lack of standard amenities – especially the absence of indoor sanitation and bathrooms.

Owners were naturally unwilling to speculate the small savings of a lifetime upon property with little apparent hope of security of investment let alone of improved return. Too often the residents' first question to the survey team was 'are you going to pull our house down?'.

The reasons were already apparent from the 1968 study. Bridgegate had always been slightly separated from the main trading centre of the town; hence its continuation in primarily residential use. But the construction of the Grosvenor Bridge, deflecting the main entry to the town away from Bridgegate and, more recently, the incorporation of this route into an inner relief road had undoubtedly increased its isolation. Although this meant that the area retained its original picturesque character, most of the buildings seemed too far gone to make restoration worthwhile. Once such a trend has started, blight can descend and spread rapidly from individual units to whole streets and neighbourhoods.

In this negative situation, the area had no natural resilience against two specific pressures upon it. The first was the County Council's requirement for more office space close to County Hall and the Castle, which they occupied. This had resulted in a policy of acquiring and 'stockpiling' property, which then remained unused or in short-term use, receiving only minimum maintenance. The second pressure was a long-standing planning permission given for redevelopment of a major site in the heart of Bridgegate. Here blighted buildings were seen as a clear indicator of an alien future.

On the positive side, enquiries from estate agents pointed to encouraging prospects for reconditioned buildings in Bridgegate.

3.4 Progress

3.4.1 *Acquiring key properties*

Possibly the most important finding of the 1971 Survey had been to identify 'key' buildings, whose preservation or return to use was vital to retain the identity of the whole area. These were buildings which by virtue of their quality and situation were of the essence and character of Bridgegate, but were in such a critical state as to be totally unattractive to private investment except for clearance and redevelopment. The sole hope for their future was for the local authority to take them over and restore them and set an example. Following the consultants' recommendation therefore, and having confirmed that the existing owners were themselves unable to take action on the problems of

Plates 16a and 17a Parts of the west side of Lower Bridge Street in about 1820, with The Falcon on the right

these buildings, the City Council commenced negotiations for the purchase of the following:

3 and 5 Shipgate St,
90 and 92 Lower Bridge St,
86 and 88 Lower Bridge St,
13 Castle St and Salvation Army premises,
25 Castle St and tyre depot,

to which were subsequently added:

Gamul House,
Gamul Place and Terrace,
5 Castle St.

A strong preference towards acquiring these properties by agreement between the District Valuer and the owners, rather than by recourse to statutory powers, resulted in complex and delicate negotiations which were sometimes protracted. Nevertheless, this policy has proved successful, not least in establishing the spirit of co-operation which has been so successfully maintained throughout the Action Programme.

3.4.2 Consultations with owners

The Survey had isolated two areas with an uncertain future arising from undeclared policies by their present owners – one in Lower Bridge Street (a private developer) and one in Shipgate Street (Cheshire County Council). As recommended, consultations with these owners were next initiated by the City Council and the consultants. Quick results could not be expected and indeed one of these major problems as yet remains unsolved. But the 'lines of communication' were opened and they remain so, in a spirit of active co-operation and understanding about mutual policies and problems.

3.4.3 Action Area working party

In 1972 an ad hoc working party of officers was set up and met at regular intervals (usually monthly, or fortnightly when circumstances made this desirable) to discuss problems and possibilities and to keep everyone in touch with current progress.

The basic working party consisted of representatives of the legal advisor, valuer, financial advisor and conservation officer, and the consultants. Guidance has been given throughout the period by representatives from the DOE London and Manchester offices. Representatives from the City Housing Department (and latterly from the County Architect's and County Highways Departments) and the local organiser of Community Service Work were invited to take part when discussing topics of particular interest to them. Close contact has been maintained with DOE's Directorate of Ancient Monuments and Historic Buildings in London.

The working party was able to bring together, in a relatively informal but effective way, the many people involved in the implementation of a Conservation Action Programme. It was able quickly to reach decisions which a less direct contact might have taken many weeks to achieve.

Minutes of meetings provided a useful record of the main aspects of the Programme, but were found to be too slow for day-to-day requirements. A system of Action Cards was therefore devised. A card was kept for each building, giving a brief description and particulars of its use, ownership and basic data. Columns were provided for action, noting by whom and when this was required. Copies were issued immediately after each meeting to all persons concerned. These Action Cards in turn formed the basis of the agenda for the next meeting.

3.4.4 The consultants' role

The role of the consultants has largely been that of a catalyst to promote consultation and action. For example, under the terms of their contract they were able to carry out surveys and feasibility studies up to sketch-design stage for any building or site in the area, whether or not this was in Council ownership. Thus, if a private owner of perhaps limited means could be persuaded to carry out conversion works, a scheme could be prepared in outline. When City acquisition of any properties became reasonably certain, the consultants were again able to prepare proposals.

3.4.5 Action Area model

A model of the area was made at a scale of 1:250. This has been most useful in giving a clear understanding of the area's varied levels and three-dimensional form, providing a far better 'feeling' than any plan could possibly convey. It has a special value in testing planning applications for

Plate 18a The model of the Action Area, viewed from the north

Costed proposals were included, both for properties which were coming into City ownership and for privately-owned buildings. Very much higher budgets for grant-aid, along with a new grant under the 1972 Town and Country Planning (Amendment) Act, were now available.

The Report noted that three disused churches within the Area had formally been declared redundant. Recommendations were therefore made for their future use and care, including a first idea for the use of St. Michael's as an exhibition centre.

Further statutory listing was recommended for previously unprotected buildings and attention was drawn to opportunities for environmental improvements.

To deal with the increasing volume of work within both the Bridgegate Action Area and the overall City conservation area, it was recommended that a technical assistant and clerk of works should be appointed to aid the conservation officer and these appointments were made shortly afterwards.

A news-sheet was delivered to every household in Bridgegate explaining the proposals for the Area, and inviting anyone who was interested in discussing the plans to contact the consultants or the conservation officer. In some cases this 'inside knowledge' has enabled valuable adjustments to be made to the preliminary proposals.

new infill buildings. Applicants are asked to submit a block model of any proposal at the same scale as the main one. The model of the new building is set in place so that its relationship to adjacent properties and its overall effect on the area can be judged through a modelscope. The planning team can then assess its suitability and discuss with the developer any desirable alteration to the massing and grouping.

3.4.6 *Involving owners and residents*
Besides those buildings which were in such danger that the Council was compelled to acquire them, there were many in Bridgegate requiring less work, or whose owners could afford the necessary repairs if given grant aid. The Council's booklet *Financial Aid for Listed Buildings* was available to anyone prepared to take the initiative, and in Bridgegate a copy was delivered to every property. In addition, the conservation officer and/or the consultant visited as many owners as possible to explain the conservation grants and to encourage them to arrange for work to be done, thereby opening up ready and informal exchange of ideas with the local people. This informal attitude has encouraged private developers to discuss projects at the planning application stage and avoid head-on conflicts later.

3.5 Bridgegate Action Programme: Interim Report No. 2*

The most important function of the Second Interim Report was to present to the City Council a detailed plan for the Action Area. The plan was approved and immediately given maximum publicity in the City and elsewhere. In retrospect, this move can be recognised as the most significant step in the entire programme. Concerted action could now begin.

3.6 The 1976 Conservation Review Study†

In 1976 an external re-survey of all the buildings within the walled City was carried out so that the present state of the buildings could be directly compared with their condition during the original survey in 1967. It was thereby possible to ascertain which repairs, alterations or conversions had been carried out and what changes had taken place in ownership, occupation and use. There was a greater need for the survey in other parts of the historic town, since detailed information on the Bridgegate area was already available from the Interim Reports. Nevertheless it was found that five buildings in the Bridgegate Action Area needed first aid or repair within three years. Another eight in the Action Area required repair within five years and fourteen were found to be deteriorating.

The five first-priority buildings were The Falcon, at the top of Lower Bridge Street, three historic houses opposite Bridge Place – Ye Olde Edgar, The Bear and Billet and Nos. 90–92 Lower Bridge Street – and No. 5 Castle Street. The 1967 survey had revealed that they were all deteriorating and, although repair and conversion schemes had been prepared for three of them, none had been started. The eight in the second priority category comprised Nos. 2 and 5 Gamul Terrace, 6 Gamul Place and Nos. 1–3, 9, 22, 23, and 25 Castle Street: in every case their condition had declined since the 1967 survey. The remaining fourteen, which were to be kept under supervision in case they too began to deteriorate more rapidly, virtually line the upper part of Lower Bridge Street.

The survey identified four areas where problems were particularly acute. Two of these were in the Action Area: Shipgate Street and Nos. 26 to 42 Lower Bridge Street. Both had been the subject of redevelopment proposals which had come to nothing leaving empty and decaying properties in their wake. The histories of these two areas are set out in detail in Chapter 4. A satisfactory outcome remains to be achieved.

Bridgegate Action Programme: Interim Report No. 2 Donald W. Insall & Associates, February 1973.

†*Chester: Conservation Review Study: 1976* Chester City Council

3.7 The 1977 floorspace survey

A feature which had emerged from both the Pilot and Review Studies was the large number of buildings whose upper floors were unused and therefore susceptible to deterioration. This problem was again highlighted the following year in a detailed floorspace survey of the city centre which formed part of the County Council's Structure Plan. Whereas buildings in the central Rows had become vacant because of the legal or financial difficulties of leasing, the main cause in Lower Bridge Street was the poor condition of the buildings themselves. Since this resulted in whole buildings, rather than just the upper floors, becoming unoccupied, opportunities arose for a more rational use of the accommodation.

The survey revealed that, although the number of partially empty properties had been reduced from five to three in the period 1967 to 1977, those which were completely unoccupied had increased from eight to twelve. This was despite the fact that five others, including The Falcon, Gamul House and Ye Old Edgar, were unoccupied for the encouraging reason that work on their repair was imminent or actually in progress. Map No. 2 compares the 1967 and 1977 situations.

MAP No. 2 Comparison of vacant properties in Lower Bridge Street, 1967 and 1977

3.8 Investment*

The amount of both public and private investment has varied considerably from year to year, as can be seen from Graph Nos. 1 and 2. The first shows how much of the Conservation Fund was awarded annually within the Action Area compared with the allocation for the entire City, and the second gives a breakdown of the different types of public and private investment annually within the Bridgegate area.

*The financial details given in this chapter and in subsequent tables are taken from information available at the beginning of 1980, and some of them—particularly for the later years–are subject to amendment.

The lower part of Graph No. 1 indicates how the original impetus of the Conservation Fund reached £100,000 in 1975, but because of general financial stringencies, fell away to about half that figure within three years. Although the City Fund was increased four-fold in April 1980, the value in real terms is only the same as that of five years previously – and about half as much again as the first year's allocation of £29,000. The upper part of the graph shows that in 1975 there was a marked peak, which is again being approached.

The effect of inflation is also clearly shown on Graph No. 2; although more Historic Building grant aid was distributed within the Action Area in 1979 than in 1975, the

MAP No. 3 Grant aid, 1972-79

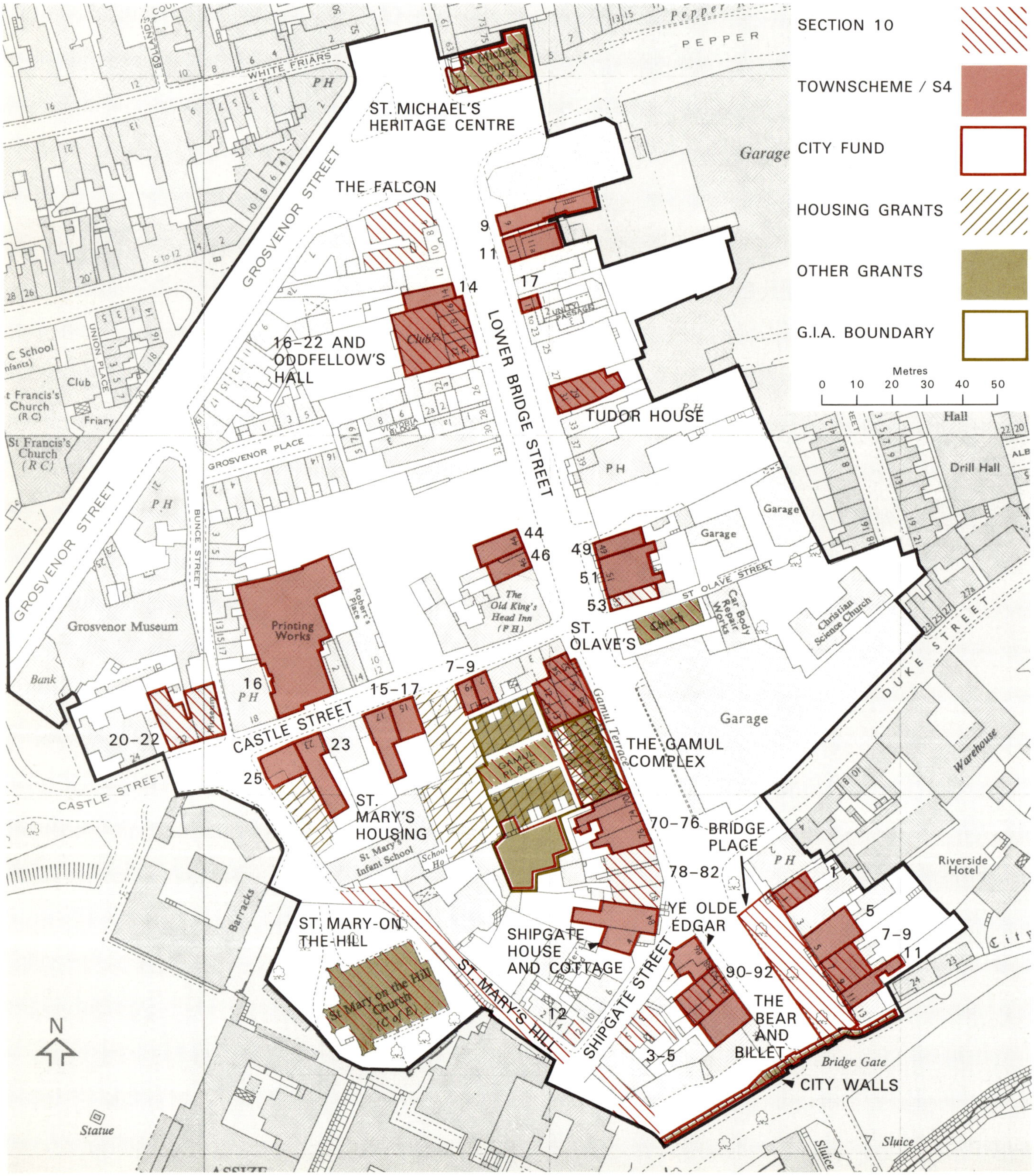

GRAPH No. 1 City conservation fund allocation 1971-80

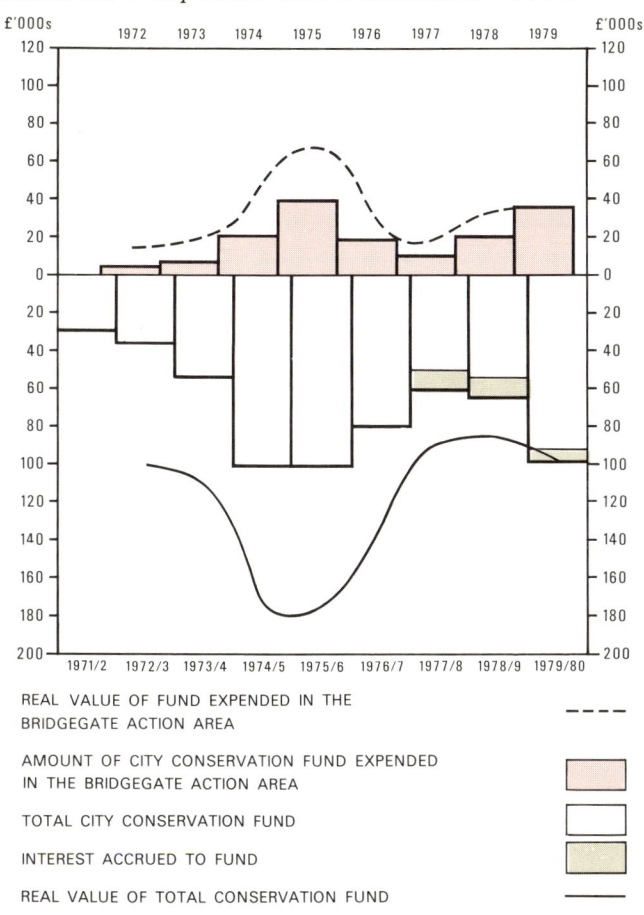

GRAPH No. 2 Grants and other investment expended in the Bridgegate Action Area, 1972-79.
NB: The graph excludes Nos. 2-6 Gamul Terrace and Nos. 1-11 Gamul Place as this scheme did not receive an Historic Building Grant

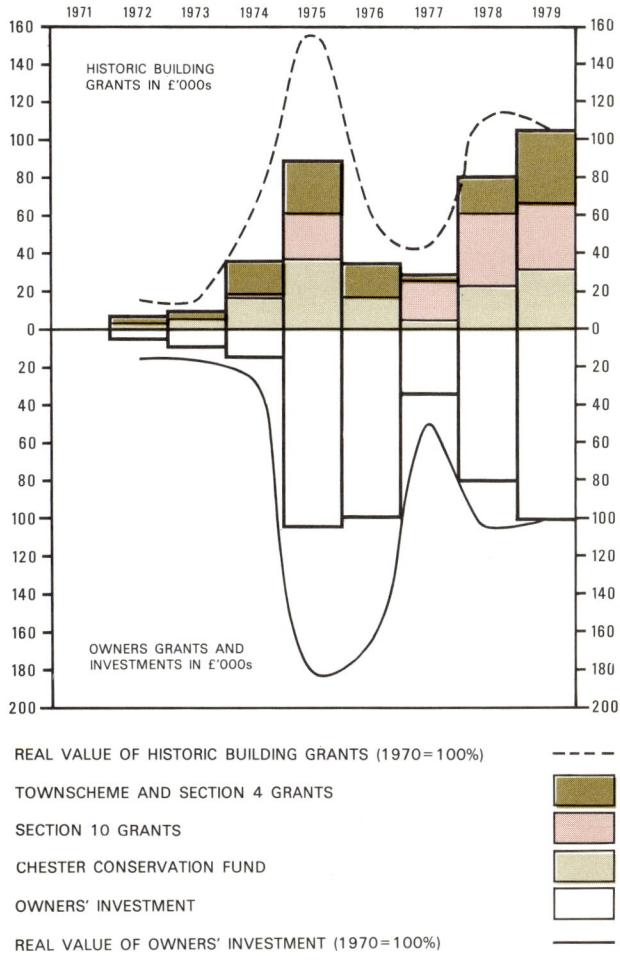

- - - - REAL VALUE OF FUND EXPENDED IN THE BRIDGEGATE ACTION AREA

▨ AMOUNT OF CITY CONSERVATION FUND EXPENDED IN THE BRIDGEGATE ACTION AREA

▢ TOTAL CITY CONSERVATION FUND

▨ INTEREST ACCRUED TO FUND

—— REAL VALUE OF TOTAL CONSERVATION FUND

- - - - REAL VALUE OF HISTORIC BUILDING GRANTS (1970=100%)

▨ TOWNSCHEME AND SECTION 4 GRANTS

▨ SECTION 10 GRANTS

▨ CHESTER CONSERVATION FUND

▢ OWNERS' INVESTMENT

—— REAL VALUE OF OWNERS' INVESTMENT (1970=100%)

TABLE No. 1 The total investment in the Bridgegate Action Area for each calendar year, 1972–79, and (in italics) the real value of that investment at 1979 prices based on the Building Tender Price Index of the Directorate of Quantity Surveying Services of the PSA

Year and % increase to update to 1979 prices	Section 10	Town Scheme & Section 4	City Conservation Fund	Total HB grants	Other grants	Owners' contributions	Total
1972		2,831	3,216	**6,047**	1,155	5,662	**12,864**
+188%		*8,154*	*9,262*	*17,416*	*3,326*	*16,306*	*37,048*
1973		2,519	5,387	**7,906**		8,541	**16,447**
+103%		*5,114*	*10,935*	*16,049*		*17,338*	*33,387*
1974	403	17,606	18,355	**36,364**	1,000	14,762	**52,126**
+75%	*705*	*30,811*	*32,121*	*63,637*	*1,750*	*25,834*	*91,221*
1975	24,788	27,855	37,050	**89,693**	51,063	171,352	**312,108**
+75%	*43,379*	*48,746*	*64,838*	*156,963*	*89,360*	*299,866*	*546,189*
1976		17,632	17,632	**35,264**	1,600	101,924	**138,788**
+66%		*29,269*	*29,269*	*58,538*	*2,656*	*169,194*	*230,388*
1977	20,458	3,651	4,273	**28,382**		35,394	**63,776**
+48%	*30,278*	*5,403*	*6,324*	*42,005*		*52,383*	*94,388*
1978	21,409	36,827	25,294	**83,530**	2,640	77,437	**163,607**
+30%	*27,832*	*47,875*	*32,882*	*108,589*	*3,432*	*100,668*	*212,689*
1979	35,516	37,271	31,652	**104,439**		101,726	**206,165**
–	*35,516*	*37,271*	*31,652*	*104,439*		*101,726*	*206,165*
Total	102,574	146,192	142,859	**391,625**	57,458	516,798	**965,881**
Total 1979 equiv.	*137,710*	*212,643*	*217,283*	*567,636*	*100,524*	*783,315*	*1,451,475*

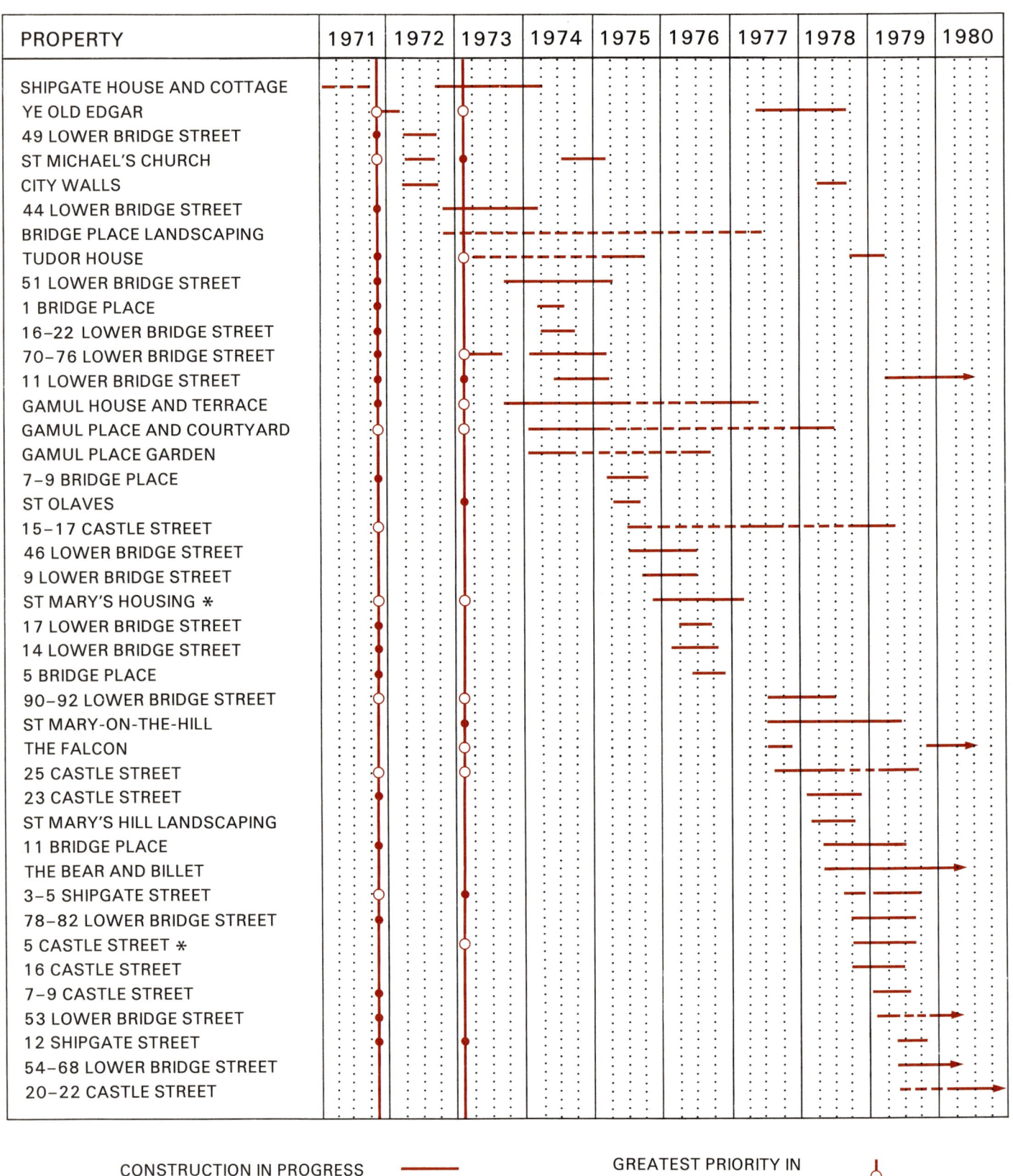

PROPERTY	1971	1972	1973	1974	1975	1976	1977	1978	1979	1980
SHIPGATE HOUSE AND COTTAGE										
YE OLD EDGAR										
49 LOWER BRIDGE STREET										
ST MICHAEL'S CHURCH										
CITY WALLS										
44 LOWER BRIDGE STREET										
BRIDGE PLACE LANDSCAPING										
TUDOR HOUSE										
51 LOWER BRIDGE STREET										
1 BRIDGE PLACE										
16–22 LOWER BRIDGE STREET										
70–76 LOWER BRIDGE STREET										
11 LOWER BRIDGE STREET										
GAMUL HOUSE AND TERRACE										
GAMUL PLACE AND COURTYARD										
GAMUL PLACE GARDEN										
7–9 BRIDGE PLACE										
ST OLAVES										
15–17 CASTLE STREET										
46 LOWER BRIDGE STREET										
9 LOWER BRIDGE STREET										
ST MARY'S HOUSING ✱										
17 LOWER BRIDGE STREET										
14 LOWER BRIDGE STREET										
5 BRIDGE PLACE										
90–92 LOWER BRIDGE STREET										
ST MARY-ON-THE-HILL										
THE FALCON										
25 CASTLE STREET										
23 CASTLE STREET										
ST MARY'S HILL LANDSCAPING										
11 BRIDGE PLACE										
THE BEAR AND BILLET										
3–5 SHIPGATE STREET										
78–82 LOWER BRIDGE STREET										
5 CASTLE STREET ✱										
16 CASTLE STREET										
7–9 CASTLE STREET										
53 LOWER BRIDGE STREET										
12 SHIPGATE STREET										
54–68 LOWER BRIDGE STREET										
20–22 CASTLE STREET										

CONSTRUCTION IN PROGRESS ———

DESIGN WORK - - - -

CONSTRUCTION CONTINUING INTO 1980 ——→

GREATEST PRIORITY IN BRIDGEGATE REPORTS

SECONDARY PRIORITY IN BRIDGEGATE REPORTS

✱ These schemes did not receive grant aid

value of this increase was entirely eliminated by the 75% rise in building costs. However, the most significant aspect of this graph – and possibly of the whole exercise – is the inference which can be drawn from the lower section. Here we see the dramatic way in which property owners in the Study Area responded to the increased availability of assistance in restoring their buildings. The line giving the real value of their investment shows a slight delay in their appreciating this opportunity. But once they realised the benefits of the grant system, their reaction was quite remarkable and very encouraging. The graph also indicates that, after the lull in 1977, local people were at this time quick to seize the opportunity as more money became available.

As the Conservation Fund allocation in both Bridgegate and the whole of Chester shows a roughly similar pattern, and as DOE grants have been available for the whole of the conservation area in the same way as in the Action Area, there is good reason to believe that the response of the people of Bridgegate is typical of the rest of Chester – or indeed anywhere else where conservation grants are made available and suitably promoted.

This study therefore shows, in microcosm, how extremely successful the present policy of grant-aid can be. Given an injection of public sector help, a great deal of conversion and repair work can be carried through, because grant aid provides an opportunity to release the latent value in property.

The forty-one grant schemes described in Chapter 6 cover nearly eighty properties and four open areas: their distribution is shown on Map No. 3. The different types of Historic Building grant* were allocated as follows:

	Type of grant				
	Section 10 (DOE)	Section 4 (DOE)	Town Scheme (DOE)	City Funds	Total HBG
No. of Schemes	19	1	24	32	40
Amount of grant	£102,574	£34,892	£111,300	£142,859	£391,625

Most schemes have therefore received more than one form of grant. Five of them enjoyed both Town Scheme and Section 10 grants, as well as help from the City Conservation Fund. Another twenty-six received only one form of grant in addition to the Fund – nineteen Town Scheme, six Section 10 and one Section 4. Of the remaining nine schemes, eight received only a Section 10 grant and one an allocation from the Fund. Of the four landscaping schemes, three were helped by Section 10 grants and two by the City Conservation Fund.

One further scheme, not itemised above, comprising 16 properties – Gamul Place and Gamul Terrace – did not receive an Historic Building Grant but benefited from a housing subsidy. The properties were made the subject of a General Improvement Area, which meant that an environmental grant was also available.

Several other forms of aid were received. St. Mary's housing development, like the Gamul housing, obtained a central government subsidy. (As this subsidy was for new development, it is not shown in the tables of expenditure in this report). Cheshire County Council contributed to the cost of landscaping Gamul Place garden and received a grant from the Manpower Services Commission for restoring the monuments in St. Mary-on-the-Hill. The area also benefited from 'Operation Eyesore' – the Special Environmental Assistance Scheme of the early 1970s – with help towards the cost of cleaning the stonework to the Chester Heritage Centre, St. Olave's Literacy Centre and the City Walls.

3.9 Current proposals

3.9.1 Groups of buildings

Following the consultants' 1978 proposals, the rehabilitation and redevelopment of the housing on each side of Shipgate Street is likely to be the next major scheme to be built in the Bridgegate Area. On the north side of the street, the city invited the involvement of a Housing Association. On the south, a scheme integrating the County Council's garages will enable the construction of an attractive residential development facing south over the River Dee; it is hoped to explore and display some of the opportunities available here with the use of models and to attract a developer who is prepared to carry the proposals forward. He may also be invited to rehabilitate the north side.

Around the corner in Lower Bridge Street the houses owned by the County (Nos. 78–82), which have remained empty for so long, are likely to be rebuilt. Their facades will be either retained or rebuilt in replica, as stipulated in the current planning consent.

3.9.2 Individual buildings

Repair work is continuing. Thanks to the creation of a special Trust, The Falcon is now open (see Case Study 5.10), and Nos. 20–22 Castle Street have been completed and are used by the Museum. Completion of work on the shop units below Gamul Terrace means that the whole Gamul complex, the most comprehensive project in the Action Area, has been brought to a successful conclusion. Work on The Bear and Billet is now complete.

3.9.3 Environmental improvement

Since the lighting in Lower Bridge Street was rather harsh and unattractive, the County Council installed more suitable standards and fittings, and added wall-mounted lamps where possible. The consultants have recommended further improvements to minimise the effects of glare and to concentrate the lighting on the more outstanding buildings. They have also suggested emphasising the city's public image by floodlighting key buildings and monuments, as has been done in other important historic cities here and on the continent.

3.10 Outstanding problems

3.10.1 Groups of buildings

The major problem is the 'gap' site Nos. 26 to 42 Lower Bridge Street. Earlier proposals were for an hotel development of a very intensive character. By 1973, although the economic climate was still favourable, a more conservation orientated approach led the City to demand the retention of the existing facades. With the bankruptcy of the development company the site came into the hands of the Offical Receiver. Several developers have since expressed an interest, and an attempt is again being made to secure a scheme appropriate in scale and detail for this key site. Although several buildings have had to be demolished

*'Historic Building grants' are abbreviated in the Tables to HBG

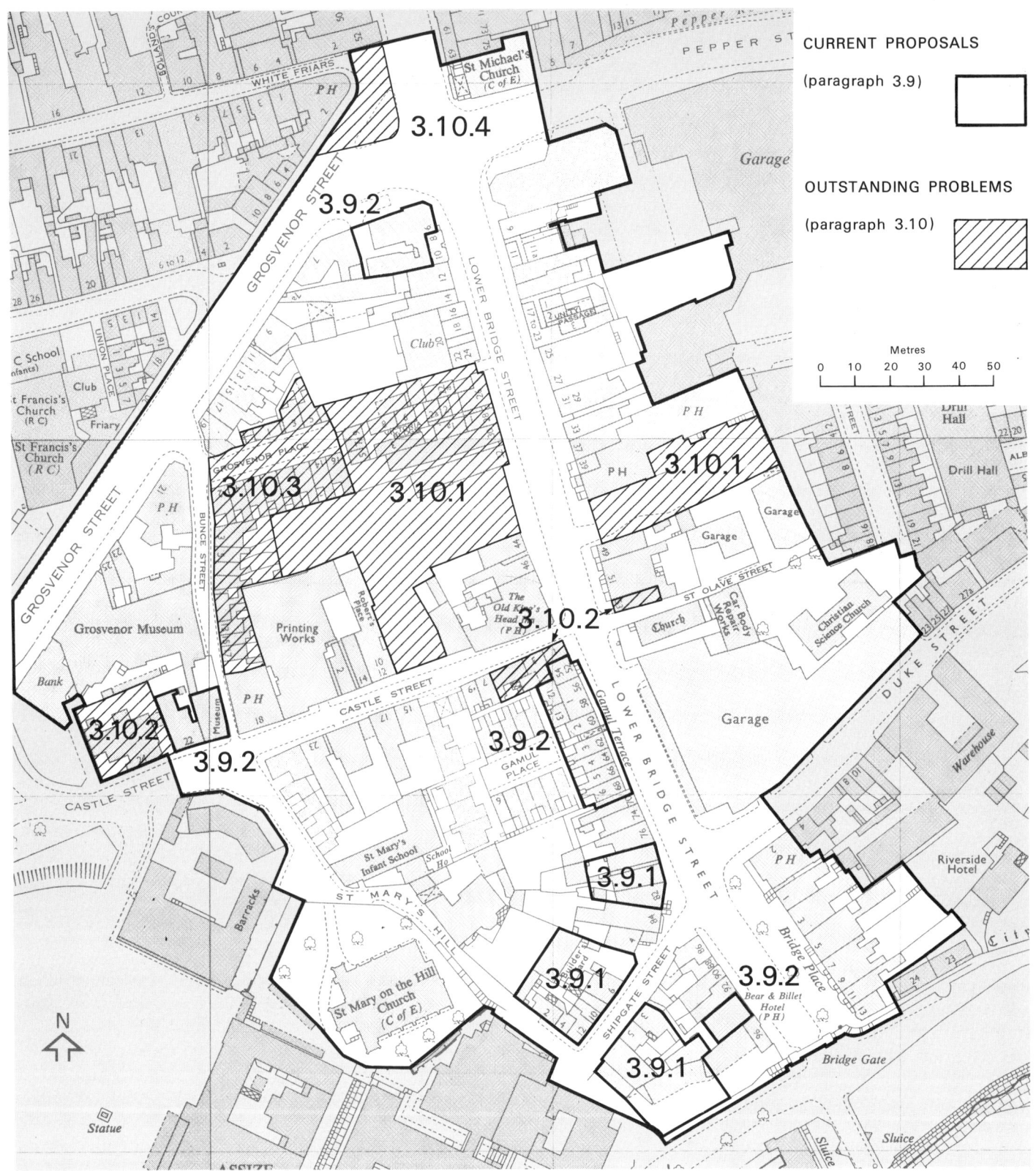

CURRENT PROPOSALS
(paragraph 3.9)

OUTSTANDING PROBLEMS
(paragraph 3.10)

MAP No. 4 Current proposals and outstanding problems (31 December 1979).

because they were unsafe, every effort is being made to keep those that remain. Efforts are also being made to prevent the effect of blight occurring beyond the site limits.

A corresponding though smaller 'gap' site exists almost directly opposite on the east side of Lower Bridge Street (Nos. 43–47). Although feasibility studies have been prepared by the consultants, there is still no firm proposal for the development of this site.

3.10.2 Individual buildings

At the corner of Castle Street, opposite the historic Ye Olde King's Head hotel, stands a Georgian building (No. 1 Castle Street) in use as a shop. This is an important corner site in

the heart of the Bridgegate area, but it presents major problems because of its poor condition and because its shop windows are out of character with the building and its surroundings. A more appropriate shopfront would greatly improve this part of the Action Area, particularly since the City Council is committed in the 1981 District Local Plan to maintaining the general character of the shops in Lower Bridge Street. Nos. 3 and 5 are not yet restored.

Another fine building needing attention is No. 24 Castle Street. Its front elevation, which may have been designed by Harrison, is now marred by some inappropriate additions. The consultants have urged the owners – the DOE Property Services Agency – to restore the building.

No. 53 Lower Bridge Street presents a further problem. The opportunity to repair this building seemed remote. But renewed steps are now being taken to bring it back into use and work is now at an advanced stage. The history of the property is outlined in Case Study 5.3.

3.10.3 Conserving residential use

Like many other towns, Chester has for years suffered a decline in its central population. The St. Mary's housing scheme and the rescue of Gamul Place and Terrace have helped to offset this trend in the Bridgegate area. In its 1981 District Plan, the City Council has also committed itself to maintaining residential uses in the area, but there remain some pockets of housing both inside the Action Area and behind the east frontage of Lower Bridge Street which call for improvement and protection from blight and commercial pressures. Rising demand for the small amount of available town centre accommodation make them particularly worthy of conservation since they are in pleasant and secluded areas largely free from traffic noise. The modest terraces in Bunce Street and Grosvenor Place are in the process of being improved by their owners now that the threat of commercial development as part of the 'hotel site' in Lower Bridge Street has been removed. Four cottages in Bunce Street may soon be renovated, two of them for Council tenants and the others for private occupation.

3.10.4 Environmental improvement

The consultants have suggested that the character of Lower Bridge Street could benefit from widening of the pavement wherever possible. This would also enable the planting of trees to minimise the impact of certain buildings whilst emphasising those more characteristic of the area.

The 'gap' sites at Nos. 26–42 and 43–47 Lower Bridge Street have already been mentioned, but a further unfortunate break in the street elevation occurs at the junction of Grosvenor Street and Bridge Street. In the 1968 Study the consultants noted the unsatisfactory relationship of Grosvenor Street with the city's gridiron plan and the opportunity which existed to endow the route with buildings worthy of its importance. This opportunity still exists.

Repaving schemes have greatly improved Bridge Place and St. Mary's Hill, but more needs to be done, possibly in Castle Street when the remaining properties in Castle Street have been restored. The consultants recommend that underground services be grouped to minimise any future damage to stone surfaces. They would like to experiment with a single duct along which pipes and wires could be threaded and withdrawn without excavation of the road surface. But clearly the cost implications would need to be very carefully considered.

Plate 26a The Action Area from the south

4 Tour of progress

During the years 1972 to 1979 grant aid has been used to encourage restoration of a total of over 70 properties, as well as contributing towards four landscaping schemes in the Bridgegate Action Area. The following is a perambulation through the area describing the buildings and the work that has been done on them. In some cases only minor work involving a few hundred pounds has been needed, but elsewhere the condition of the building has required many thousands, often from a wide variety of sources. Where the means found to solve these problems are of general interest and could be applied elsewhere the tour has been interspersed with more detailed comment.

MAP No. 5 Tour of progress

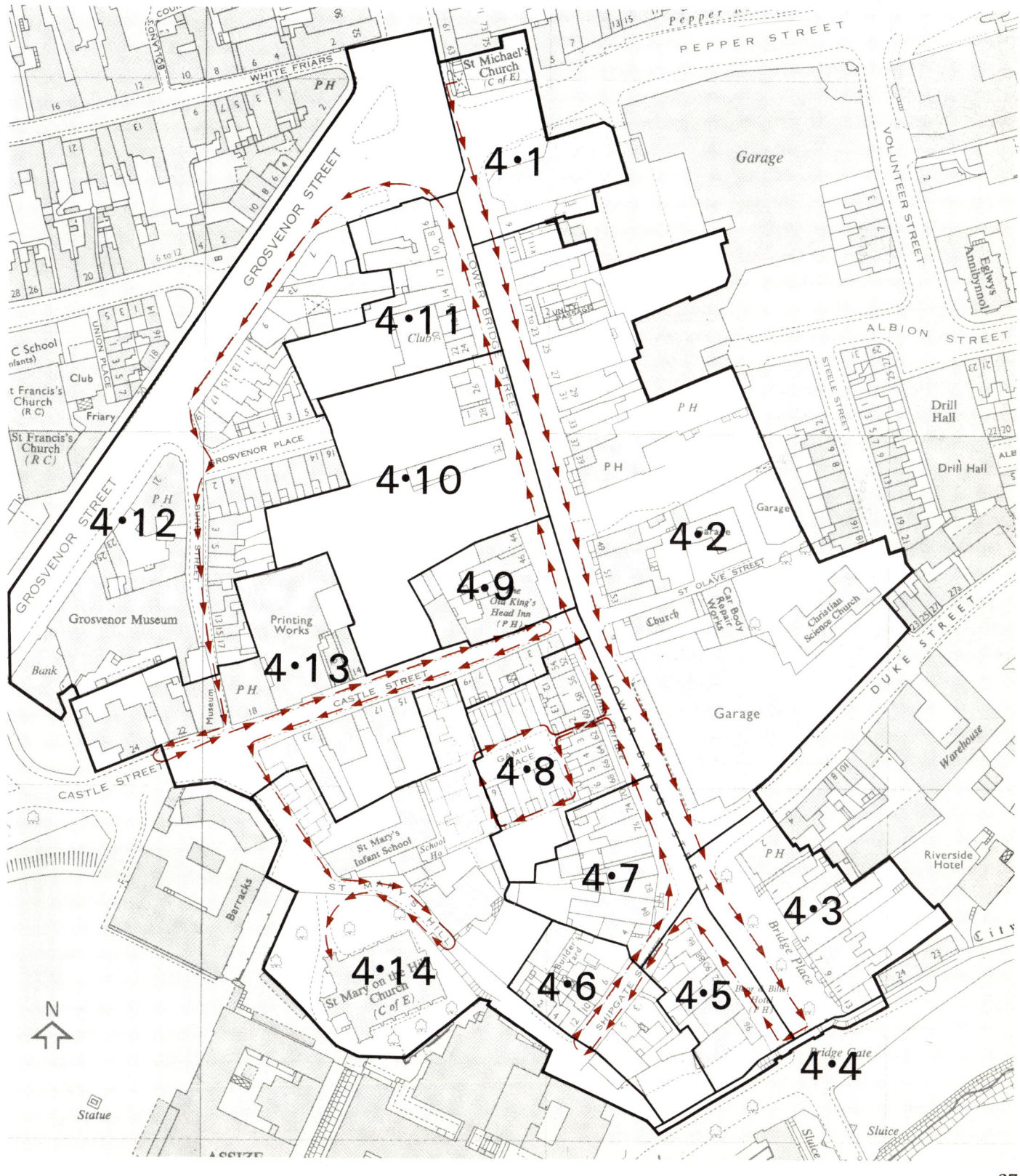

Plate 28a The Red Lion site before redevelopment

Certain properties selected for full case-studies are included in Chapter 5. One case-history forms the subject of Chapter 6. The perambulation, whose route is shown on Map No. 5, includes 41 grant-aided schemes.

Following the details of each building or area is a table showing the grants allocated over the past ten years.

Column 1 shows the year in which the grant money was paid or, in some cases, agreed.

Columns 2–5 indicate the extent of the grants to the nearest £. DOE grants awarded under Section 10 of the 1972 Act are shown in *Column 2;* Town Scheme (DOE) contributions and, where applicable, Section 4 grants in *Column 3;* grants awarded by the City of Chester from the City Conservation Fund in *Column 4. Column 5* gives the combined total of these 'Historic Building' grants.

Column 6 shows other grants and contributions; these include house improvement grants, General Improvement Area Environmental grants, SEAS (Special Environmental Assistance Scheme 'Operation Eyesore') grants, Manpower Services Commission grants, special contributions from the County, etc.

Column 7 gives the owner's contribution towards grant-aided schemes.

Column 8 gives the total cost of the works, including alterations, conversions and improvements. As 50 per cent grant for all aspects of the work is not available, the total shown is usually more than twice the total grant aid.

4.1 Top of Lower Bridge Street

4.1.1 *The Chester Heritage Centre*

St Michael's Church has been chosen as the starting point of this tour. It not only forms a significant landmark at a corner of what is now one of the main traffic intersections within the City Walls, but it has been converted into the City's Heritage Centre and is therefore symbolic of all the effort that has gone into the conservation of Chester over the past ten years. Details of the conversion of this church and the service it now offers are given in Case Study 5.1. Grant aid was as follows:

Years	S10	T/S	City	Total HBG	Other Grants	Owner	Total Costs	1979 Equiv.
1974						10,500[1]	**10,500**	*18,375*
1975	16,000		9,195	**25,195**	7,413[2]	2,471	**35,079**	*61,388*
Total	16,000		9,195	**25,195**	7,413	12,971	**45,579**	*79,763*

1. Acquisition cost
2. SEAS grant

4.1.2 *Windsor House*

A substantial office building dominates the top of Lower Bridge Street. This occupies an important site commanding the junction with Pepper Street and had remained ripe for development ever since 1968, when Pepper Street was widened to form part of the Inner Ring Road. Nos. 1 to 5 Lower Bridge Street had been demolished, leaving exposed a somewhat unstable flank of No. 7 – The Red Lion. The pub itself had closed and both it and No. 9 were deteriorating fast.

At the time of the 1971 Interim Report on Bridgegate, a scheme for office development on this site was under active consideration. A suggestion was made for a pedestrian bridge from St Michael's across Pepper Street to a first-floor entry at Row level in the new building; but the idea was on balance found impracticable, due mainly to the presence of complex underground services.

By 1973, promising schemes for the new office development were being submitted, and seemed likely to go ahead. Any minor features of the old building of sufficient interest (eg decorative plaster emblems and some oak

Plate 29a After redevelopment; the Chester Heritage Centre is on the left

Plate 29b An audio-visual presentation at the Chester Heritage Centre

boarding) were meanwhile salvaged by the Conservation Section before demolition work began.

Outline approval was granted in April 1973 and was followed by a full planning application for offices with a showroom at the lower ground floor level. This was approved – subject to various conditions – in September 1974. Work was started in January 1974 and the new building was completed in September 1975.

4.1.3 *No. 9 Lower Bridge Street*

Nos. 9 to 19 Lower Bridge Street are all Grade II. While individually they are not particularly important, they were listed for their group value. Work on No. 9 Lower Bridge Street was started in September 1975 and completed in 1976. Here little remained of the interiors, which had been gutted by fire, and the whole of the building was rebuilt behind a repaired facade. The accommodation now comprises a shop at ground floor, with offices and a flat above.

Year	S10	T/S	City	Total HBG	Other Grants	Owner	Total Costs	1979 Equiv.
1976		5,092	5,092	**10,184**		63,577	**73,761**	*122,443*

4.2 Lower Bridge Street: east side

Lower Bridge Street forms the spine of the Study Area, running southwards downhill to Bridgegate and the medieval Old Dee Bridge immediately beyond the City Walls. The Street used to be lined almost continuously with good tall seventeenth and eighteenth-century facades, including several important buildings. But by 1970 only the west side remained complete, an unfortunate gap having been formed on the eastern side by earlier demolition. Since then, despite all the successes within the Area, an even more disastrous gap has opened up between the buildings

GROUND FLOOR PLAN

Metres
0 1 2 3 4 5

Hairdressing Salon

W.C.
W.C.

FIRST FLOOR PLAN

Lobby | G.P.O. Room

Row Level

Reception Office 1

Entrance Hall

Office 2

SECOND FLOOR PLAN

Office 3 | F. Toilet | Staff Kitchen | Lounge/Reception

Landing

Office 4 | Store | Office 5

THIRD FLOOR PLAN

M. Toilet | Office 6

Future Board Room | Landing

Office 7

CROSS SECTION B-B

Landing

M. Toilet

Landing

Staff Kit.

Entrance Hall

Hairdressing Salon

Basement

LONGITUDINAL SECTION A-A

Office 6 | M. Toilet | Board Room

Lounge/Reception | Staff Kit. | F. Toilet | Office 3

G.P.O. Room | Entrance Hall | Lobby | Row | Level

Hairdressing Salon

Basement

Plate 30a Nos. 11 and 11A Lower Bridge Street

to the west, widening over the years as blight and decay have spread, until it forms by far the most serious problem to be resolved in the Study Area.

In the 1968 report Donald Insall noted that the shops in Lower Bridge Street were on the decline. But since then there have been many success stories, and both residents and commerce are being attracted back; the growing number of restaurants and antique shops indicates its importance as the main route from the centre down to the river.

4.2.1 No. 11 Lower Bridge Street

Next to The Red Lion site are Nos. 11 and 11A Lower Bridge Street. They form an important Georgian building with one of the few surviving Rows remaining in the Action Area. It was threatened by the widening of Pepper Street and in the 1971 Survey was noted as deteriorating and needing vigilance in view of its uncertain future.

In 1974 the property changed hands and the new owner applied for grant aid to put it into use as an antique shop with offices above and a restaurant in the cellar. The work involved reslating the roof, rebuilding the upper part of the street elevation and damp-proofing the cellar. Although the owner employed an architectural consultant, he proceeded to carry out most of the work himself with the help of a local builder. The Council were concerned about the lack of supervision, but they agreed to provide grant aid. The owner was, however, unable to complete the work and sold the property.

His successor converted the ground floor and basement into a hairdressing salon and, in 1979, sold the three upper floors as 11A Lower Bridge Street to a property company who have converted them into offices. The work involved installing toilets, central heating, re-wiring, partitions and

new rear windows. The staircase and the oak beamed ceiling to the top floor were restored, and the building is now in full use on all five floors.

Grant aid had been agreed towards the cost of repairs but, because of a dispute over the appearance of extractor vents on the front elevation, it has not yet been paid.

Year	S10	T/S	City	Total HBG	Other Grants	Owner	Total Costs	1979 Equiv.
1975		1,783	1,783	3,566		6,174	9,740	17,045

4.2.2 No. 17 Lower Bridge Street

The only other building in this group to receive grant aid was No. 17, as follows:

Year	S10	T/S	City	Total HBG	Other Grants	Owner	Total Costs	1979 Equiv.
1976		500	500	1,000		1,000	2,000	3,320

No. 25–27 is a new building with a contemporary faceted facade which gives it a vertical emphasis and reduces its scale to that of its neighbours. Next to this is a particularly fine sixteenth century timber-framed structure called Tudor House.

4.2.3 Tudor House (Nos. 29–31 Lower Bridge Street)

Although Tudor House is listed, it was until recently in an extremely dilapidated state. Details of the tortuous processes involved its restoration – which involved loans as well as grants – are given in Case Study 5.2. The financial details are as follows:

Year	S10	T/S	City[1]	Total HBG	Other Grants	Owner	Total Costs	1979 Equiv.
1975		4,737	4,737	9,474		18,748	28,222	49,389
1979	105		105	210		507	717	717
Total	105	4,737	4,842	9,684		19,255	28,939	50,106

1. The City also loaned the owner £7,220 in 1974.

The buildings from Tudor House down to the Clavertons Wine Bar, No. 33–41, are listed grade II for their group value. No. 39–41 dates from 1715 and has undergone many uses and had many names: (The Albion Hotel, Park House, the County Library and, until recently, The Talbot Hotel). It is now used partly by the Grosvenor Hotel, while the central part contains an antique market.

The vacant site next door is owned by the Grosvenor Estate and since 1976 the Insall Consultancy has produced several schemes for the owner. The disastrous effect of this gap – resulting from the demolition of Nos. 43–47 – was noted in the original report; it has spoiled the appearance of the east side of Lower Bridge Street for some twenty years.

4.2.4 No. 49 Lower Bridge Street

Beyond the gap, Nos. 49–53 form another Grade II group. No. 49 dates from the early eighteenth century and received grant-aid for minor repairs in 1972, as follows:

Year	S10	T/S	City	Total HBG	Other Grants	Owner	Total Costs	1979 Equiv.
1972		31	31	62		62	124	357

4.2.5 No. 51 Lower Bridge Street

No. 51 is a substantial four-storey eighteenth century house. In December 1973, the owners applied for aid towards reslating the roof, new gutters and downpipes, repairing the windows and rebuilding a new rear gable. By 1975 the work was completed and the grant allocated, as follows:

Year	S10	T/S	City	Total HBG	Other Grants	Owner	Total Costs	1979 Equiv.
1975		769	769	1,538		1,538	3,076	5,383

4.2.6 No. 53 Lower Bridge Street

In contrast, No. 53 is a tiny seventeenth century timber-framed house with a nineteenth century gabled front. Details of the almost insuperable problems surrounding the repair of this building are given in Case Study 5.3. The only grant money expended so far is for a detailed structural survey, as follows:

Year	S10	T/S	City	Total HBG	Other Grants	Owner	Total Costs	1979 Equiv.
1979	375		375	750			750	750

4.2.7 St Olave's Church (No. 55 Lower Bridge Street)

No. 55 was a small church, St Olave's, set back from Lower Bridge Street behind its raised forecourt. It is listed Grade II and like many of Chester's churches was much altered in the nineteenth century but still contains traces of the earlier pre-Norman Church. It was purchased by the County in May 1975 as an Adult Literacy Centre and the elevation was cleaned with the help of a grant from SEAS.

Plate 31a Nos. 41–51 Lower Bridge Street showing the gap left by the demolition of Nos. 43–47

Plate 31b Nos. 43–47 shortly before they were pulled down

Plate 32a Looking down the east side of Lower Bridge Street. (Compare this with pls. 14a and 15a)

Year	S10	T/S	City	Total HBG	Other Grants	Owner	Total Costs	1979 Equiv.
1975	5,000			5,000	750[1]	2,861	8,611	15,069

1. SEAS grant

Between St Olave's and Duke Street and taking up more than one hundred and fifty feet of frontage is a garage building whose vast bulk intrudes into the intimate scale of the rest of the Street.

4.3 Bridge Place

Further down, on the south side of Duke Street, is an attractive Victorian public house and beyond it, reaching down to the City Wall, is Bridge Place, a fine Georgian terrace. All the properties except No. 3 have recently been awarded grants.

4.3.1 No. 1 Bridge Place

In February 1974 the owner of No. 1 applied for a grant to restore the front elevation. This involved replacing six sash windows, repairing the string course and cornice and redecorating the woodwork. Grant aid was given and the work was completed by May of that year.

Year	S10	T/S	City	Total HBG	Other Grants	Owner	Total Costs	1979 Equiv.
1974	30	272	272	574		575	1,149	2,011

4.3.2 No. 5 Bridge Place

In July 1976 the City and DOE agreed to award grant aid for the restoration of No. 5 to allow it to be used as offices.

This involved considerable structural work including shoring up and underpinning the rear wall. The work was completed in November 1976, at a cost of just over £11,000.

Year	S10	T/S	City	Total HBG	Other Grants	Owner	Total Costs	1979 Equiv.
1976		2,777	2,777	5,554		5,554	11,108	18,439

4.3.3 Nos. 7–9 Bridge Place

The previous year the City and DOE had also agreed to contribute towards the cost of replacing the sash windows and repairing the entrance door to Nos. 7–9.

Year	S10	T/S	City	Total HBG	Other Grants	Owner	Total Costs	1979 Equiv.
1975	63	214	214	491		492	983	1,720

4.3.4 No. 11 Bridge Place

Towards the end of 1977, the owner of No. 11 applied for grant aid to enable him to reslate and roof and eradicate an outbreak of wet-rot and beetle attack. The request was granted and the work carried out during the following two years.

Year	S10	T/S	City	Total HBG	Other Grants	Owner	Total Costs	1979 Equiv.
1979		1,603	1,603	3,206		3,206	6,412	6,412

4.3.5 Bridge Place landscaping

The houses along Bridge Place are set back from the Street and separated from it by a row of mature trees and an attractive cobbled forecourt. For many years the area had

32

Plates 33a and 33b   Bridge Place before and after the landscaping

been marred by parked cars, and it had often been suggested that this should be prevented.

In November 1972, the Insall consultancy prepared a scheme for improving the forecourt. This entailed removing the cars and providing residents with parking spaces nearby. All the residents were visited and shown the scheme and their views were sought. The consultants found that most of the cars parked on the cobbles belonged not to the residents but to shoppers and office workers. All but one of the residents were in favour of the scheme, although some had security reservations about alternative parking on the Roodee.

The County Highways Department (who now have responsibility for all roads, including those in the City) agreed to the enhancement scheme provided the City Council agreed to undertake the future cleaning and maintenance. Works included relaying paving and setts and installing seats and bollards. A tree was donated by a City Councillor.

Year	S10	T/S	City	Total HBG	Other Grants	Owner	Total Costs	1979 Equiv.
1977	208		622	**830**		830	**1,660**	*2,457*

4.4 The City Walls at Bridgegate

Chester owes much of its special character and identity to its City Walls. Although the Council ensures that they are adequately maintained, a section at Bridgegate was discovered in 1972 to be in poor condition. Some emergency work has now been done and a full survey of the Walls has since been prepared by the City Conservation Section.

Stonework cleaning has received financial assistance from the Government's Special Environmental Assistance Scheme which was operational only in 1972.

Year	S10	T/S	City	Total HBG	Other Grants	Owner	Total Costs	1979 Equiv.
1972		385		**385**	1,155[1]		**1,540**	*4,435*
1978	1,500			**1,500**			**1,500**	*1,950*
Total	1,500	385		**1,885**	1,155		**3,040**	*6,385*

1. SEAS grant

4.5 Nos. 96–86 Lower Bridge Street

4.5.1 *The Bear and Billet (No. 94 Lower Bridge Street)**

The perambulation now continues up the west side of Lower Bridge Street, starting with the group between the Bridge and Shipgate Street. The Bear and Billet is an outstanding Grade I black and white house. Details of its restoration, which was completed early in 1980, are given in Case Study 5.4.

Year	S10	S4	City	Total HBG	Other Grants	Owner	Total Costs	1979 Equiv.
1977						2,209	**2,209**	*3,269*
1978	9,855	4,927		**14,782**		12,131	**26,913**	*34,987*
1979	25,037	11,073		**36,110**		12,421	**48,531**	*48,531*
Total	34,892	16,000		**50,892**		26,761	**77,653**	*86,787*

4.5.2 *The Three Kings Studios (Nos. 90–92 Lower Bridge Street)*

No. 90–92, next door, is a plain early nineteenth century

* On-going scheme.

Plate 34a The lower end of Bridgegate at the time of the 1968 report

Plate 34b Ye Olde Edgar and the derelict properties on the south side of Shipgate Street

building listed Grade II, which has been converted into a house and pottery studio. The story of its restoration is particularly interesting and is therefore set out in detail in Chapter 6.

Year	S10	T/S	City	Total HBG	Other Grants	Owner	Total Costs	1979 Equiv.
1977						9,000	**9,000**	*13,320*
1978	15,000	6,562	6,562	**28,124**		12,500	**40,624**	*52,811*
Total	15,000	6,562	6,562	**28,124**		21,500	**49,624**	*66,131*

4.5.3 Ye Olde Edgar (Nos. 86–88 Lower Bridge Street)

Next door, and turning the corner into Shipgate Street, is Ye Olde Edgar, a Grade II half-timbered building which forms the subject of Case Study 5.5.

Year	S10	T/S	City	Total HBG	Other Grants	Owner	Total Costs	1979 Equiv.
1978		19,250	11,395	**30,645**		30,990	**61,635**	*80,125*

4.6 Shipgate Street

Shipgate Street was originally an old packhorse route and, compared with Lower Bridge Street, possesses a sudden and engaging miniaturisation of scale. Nos. 3 and 5 on the south side and all except No. 6 on the north are listed. Their deteriorated condition was noted in the 1968 report and has continued over the last decade.

4.6.1 Nos. 3 and 5 Shipgate Street

Nos. 3 and 5 had at one time been used as customs buildings but by 1972 they were unoccupied and the City purchased them as part of a block acquisition. A structural survey showed them to be in a dangerous condition. The collapse of the roof of No. 3 had resulted in bulging and saturated walls and the imminent collapse of the ground and first floors. Except for minor structural movement and weaknesses created by unsupported openings, No. 5 was relatively sound.

The main characteristic of No. 3, which dates from the seventeenth century, was an attractive ogee-headed doorcase. No. 5 was a nineteenth century addition. In November 1978 the consultants submitted a report* recommending that, rather than attempt a complete restoration, the facades alone should be retained and a new residential development be constructed behind them, taking up the whole site as far south as the City Walls. The report was accepted by the City early in 1979 and, to prevent the collapse of the facades while a private developer was found, Nos. 3 and 5 were shored up and an unstable chimney stack removed at a cost of £2,900.

Year	S10	T/S	City	Total HBG	Other Grants	Owner	Total Costs	1979 Equiv.
1979	2,900			**2,900**		1,400	**4,300**	*4,300*

4.6.2 No. 12 Shipgate Street

The group of houses on the north side comprises Nos. 6–12 together with Nos. 2 and 4 St Mary's Hill. They form an

* *Shipgate Street, Chester: Proposals for Revitalisation,* published jointly by the Chester City Council and Donald W. Insall and Associates. November 1978

Plate 35a Looking up St Mary's Hill from Shipgate Street

attractive townscape element and, although in poor condition, are suitable for residential use. No. 6 is a substantial Victorian building with sandstone dressings and No. 8–10, dating from the early nineteenth century, retains its original stone heads and cills. Except for the roof of No. 6, both were found to be in reasonable condition and are still occupied. Although the consultants considered No. 12 to be in a dangerous condition, with bulging and cracking walls, they thought that, because it still retained its original pedimented doorcase, stone heads and cills and sash windows, it was worth retaining. Emergency works to No. 12 were therefore undertaken with the help of S10 grant.

Year	S10	T/S	City	Total HBG	Other Grants	Owner	Total Costs	1979 Equiv.
1979	767			**767**		767	**1,534**	*1,534*

Except for No. 10 the whole block is owned by the County Council. In their report the consultants recommended that, because of their condition and quality, the houses should be extended and restored to form a modernised residential block instead of being demolished to make way for County Council offices. Both the County and City Councils have accepted the findings of the report, the City completed their purchase from the County and offered the properties on the open market for rehabilitation.

4.7 Nos. 84–70 Lower Bridge Street

4.7.1 Shipgate House and Cottage (No. 84 Lower Bridge Street and No. 4 Shipgate Street)

No. 84 Lower Bridge Street, on the north-east corner of

35

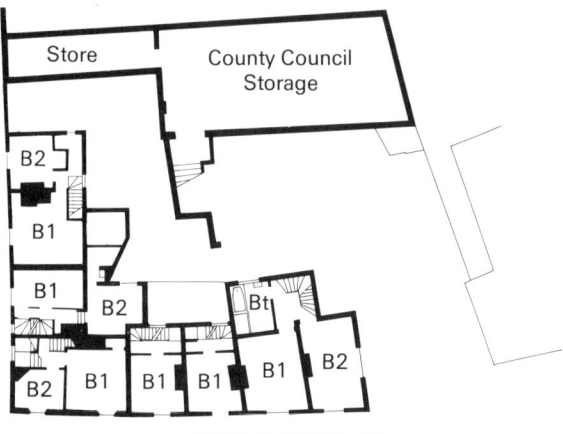

Plate 36a The north side of Shipgate Street; Nos. 3 and 5 are in the foreground

Plate 36b Proposals for the north side of Shipgate Street

S	Sitting Room	
D	Dining Room	
B	Bedroom	
K	Kitchen	
Bt	Bathroom	
O	Office	
G	Garden	
Y	Yard	
St	Stores	

0   Metres   10

FIRST FLOOR PLAN

SECOND FLOOR PLAN

GROUND FLOOR PLAN

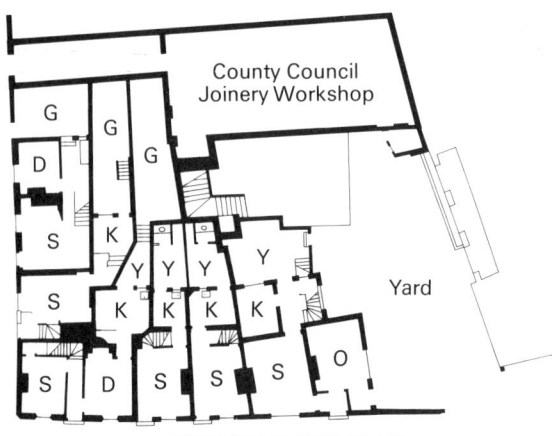

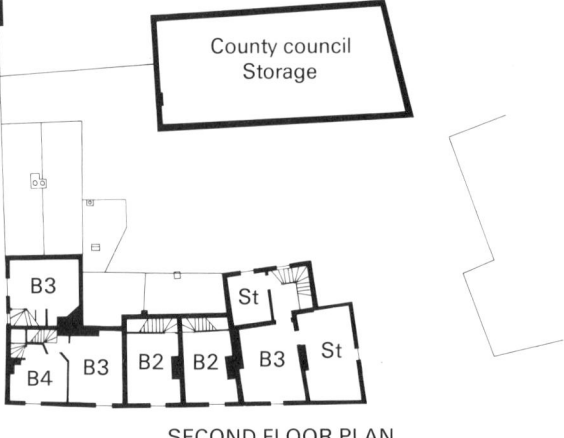

Plate 37a Shipgate House and Nos. 78–82 Lower Bridge Street

Shipgate Street, is named Shipgate House, and is an imposing 18th century building which, together with Shipgate Cottage (No. 4 Shipgate Street) next door, form the subject of Case Study 5.7.

Year	S10	T/S	1City	Total HBG	Other Grants	Owner	Total Costs	1979 Equiv.
1972		2,800	2,800	5,600		5,600	11,200	32,256
1974		325	325	650		650	1,300	2,275
1975		2,875	2,875	5,750		48,545	54,295	95,016
Total		6,000	6,000	12,000		54,795	66,795	129,547

4.7.2 Nos. 78–82 Lower Bridge Street

Nos. 94 to 70 Lower Bridge Street are listed as of group value. Nos. 70–82 form a virtually continuous facade of four-storey red brick houses climbing away from Shipgate House in a gradual curve. The first four date from the late eighteenth century while the other two were built a little later. The County had purchased several of these properties in the hope of redeveloping the whole block for their own use, but either retaining or replicating the facades. The buildings have been empty for several years and, when they were surveyed in 1978, Nos. 78–82 were found to be in a potentially dangerous condition. Extensive emergency works were therefore put in hand with the help of grant aid and the properties were then boarded up.

Year	S10	T/S	City	Total HBG	Other Grants	Owner	Total Costs	1979 Equiv.
1979	12,500			12,500		12,500	25,000	25,000

4.7.3 Nos. 70–76 Lower Bridge Street

Nos. 70 to 76 have been purchased by a local Trust and converted into offices. Details of the scheme are given in Case Study 5.8.

Year	S10	T/S	City	Total HBG	Other Grants	Owner	Total Costs	1979 Equiv.
1973		139	139	278		278	556	1,129
1974		887	887	1,774		1,774	3,548	6,209
1975		722	722	1,444		6,066	7,510	13,143
Total		1,748	1,748	3,496		8,118	11,614	20,481

4.8 The Gamul complex

Moving on up Lower Bridge Street, we now come to what is probably the most successful scheme in the Action Area, comprising not only the buildings facing onto the street, but also those in the backlands. It consists of Gamul Cottage, a row of shops (Nos. 54–68 Lower Bridge Street) over which are built Nos. 1–6 Gamul Terrace (including Gamul House), and Nos. 1–13 Gamul Place. Gamul House is Listed Grade II★. Because of its importance, the group has been made the subject of Case Study 5.9. Details of the various types of grants are given below.

Gamul House (No. 1 Gamul Terrace), Gamul Cottage (formerly No. 52 Lower Bridge Street) and Nos. 12–13 Gamul Place

Year	S10	T/S	City	Total HBG	Other Grants	Owner	Total Costs	1979 Equiv.
1973			2,868	2,868		2,868	5,736	11,644
1974		15,676	15,676	31,352			31,352	54,866
1975		14,444	14,444	28,888		9,700	38,588	67,529
1976		3,531	3,531	7,062			7,062	11,723
1977		1,949	1,949	3,898			3,898	5,769
Total		35,600	38,468	74,068		12,568	86,636	151,531

Plates 38a and 38b Gamul Terrace and House in their original condition and after repair

Nos. 1–11 Gamul Place and Nos. 2–6 Gamul Terrace

Year	S10	T/S	City	Total HBG	Other Grants	Owner	Total Costs	1979 Equiv.
1975					42,900[1]	66,410[2]	109,310	191,293

1. Central Government Housing Subsidy
2. Chester City Council Housing Revenue Account

Nos. 54–68 Lower Bridge Street (Shop Units)*

Year	S10	T/S	City	Total HBG	Other Grants	Owner	Total Costs	1979 Equiv.
1979	7,864		7,864	15,728		37,972	53,700	53,700

Gamul Place Courtyard

Year	S10	T/S	City	Total HBG	Other Grants	Owner	Total Costs	1979 Equiv.
1975	3,725			3,725		3,725	7,450	13,038
1976					1,600[1]	1,600[2]	3,200	5,312
Total	3,725			3,725	1,600	5,325	10,650	18,350

1. GIA Environmental Grant
2. Chester City Council Housing Revenue Account

Gamul Place Garden Landscaping Scheme

Year	S10	T/S	City	Total HBG	Other Grants	Owner	Total Costs	1979 Equiv.
1974			750	750	1,000[1]		1,750	3,063

1. Contribution from County Council augmented by voluntary labour (see Case Study)

4.9 Nos. 50–44 Lower Bridge Street

Immediately north of Gamul Terrace is the entrance to Castle Street, on the corner of which is another particularly valuable timber framed building, Ye Olde Kings Head. It dates from the early seventeenth century—although some parts may be earlier—and was owned by Randle Holme I, Deputy King of Arms and Mayor of Chester in 1833. For many years it has been used as an hotel and, because the building has been in continuous use and well maintained, it is the only one of its kind in the area which has not had to apply for repair grants in the last ten years.

4.9.1 *Nos. 46 and 44 Lower Bridge Street*

Originally Nos. 32 to 60 were listed Grade II for their group value, but now only two buildings, Nos. 46 and 44, separate Ye Olde Kings Head from the worst area of blight and decay in Bridgegate—26 to 42 Lower Bridge Street. The spread of this blight has been checked with the help of grant aid, £10,000 to No. 46 between 1975 and 1976, and £4,600 to No. 44 in 1973.

No. 46 Lower Bridge Street

Year	S10	T/S	City	Total HBG	Other Grants	Owner	Total Costs	1979 Equiv.
1975		1,000	1,000	2,000		2,000	4,000	7,000
1976		4,000	4,000	8,000		8,000	16,000	26,560
Total		5,000	5,000	10,000		10,000	20,000	33,560

* On-going scheme.

Plate 39a No. 44 Lower Bridge Street

No. 44 Lower Bridge Street

Year	S10	T/S	City	Total HBG	Other Grants	Owner	Total Costs	1979 Equiv.
1973		2,300	2,300	4,600		5,234	9,834	19,963

On inspection in 1971, No. 44 was found to be in severe disrepair. The brick front with its stone quoins was in reasonable condition, but a beam over the shop front had lost all its bearing at one end, the rear wall was bulging badly and first and second floor lintels were broken, while most windows were missing or damaged. The rear roof slope was devoid of slating or leadwork and weather was destroying the roof, floors and ceilings.

By 1972 it had been possible to interest a private purchaser. Two contracts were let: one for demolition work, including various derelict outbuildings, and one for restoration of the main building. The latter was commenced in November 1972 and completed in early 1974. The defective shopfront beam was replaced by steel, the upper part of the rear wall rebuilt and the roof and floors replaced using original purlins and cross-beams still in sound condition. During the work, much embedded timber was discovered in the party walls, with considerable evidence of an earlier timber framed building set further back from the street than the present building. The lock-up shop at street level provides 70 sq m of lettable space, and the three upper floors have been converted to provide 160 sq m of offices. These are all now in full use.

Plate 40a Nos. 38–42 Lower Bridge Street—now demolished

4.10 Nos. 42–26 Lower Bridge Street

We now come to the one major blot on the success story of Bridgegate, the 'Hotel Site' encompassing Nos. 26 to 42 Lower Bridge Street. A typically varied group of buildings, it included a splendid if derelict four-storey eighteenth century house with double-branched stairways to its raised entrance (Nos. 38 to 42), another good eighteenth century building entered by a characteristic tall Chester arch (Nos. 34–36) and an attractive 'black and white' facade (No. 32). Three other buildings completed the group.

In a survey carried out in 1970, it was estimated that the total cost of repairing the six buildings would be between £24,000 and £33,300 [£96,000 and £133,200]. The survey findings and the present position are as follows:

No. 26: A late Victorian building previously used as a tobacco shop but then largely derelict. The repairs to the front portion were estimated to cost between £1,000 [£4,000] and £1,500 [£6,000]. All that now remains is the shell of the building.

No. 28: A three-storey brick building with a shop at ground level. The repairs, which involved a new roof and some re-pointing, was estimated at between £1,500 [£6,000] and £1,800 [£7,200]. Only the shell now remains.

No. 30: A gabled timber-framed structure of three storeys which by 1970 was in a very poor condition. Props had been inserted to support the beams internally, and the dummy timbers painted onto the facade plaster hid the fact that the timber beneath was badly decayed. It was considered that some early Victorian tenements at the rear were beyond saving. The cost of repair was estimated at between £5,000 [£20,000] and £10,000 [£40,000]. The building was demolished in 1971.

No. 32: Another gabled building on four floors. It is listed Grade II because the late seventeenth century front was thought to hide a fifteenth century interior. The 1970 survey revealed an unusual form of floor construction in which 6–8 mm thick boards were supported directly on transverse beams. The cost of repairing the decay to the front and the roof was estimated to be between £2,000 [£8,000] and £2,500 [£10,000]. Again, only the shell remains.

No. 34 (shop unit) with No. 36 (house over): Listed Grade II, it contained a spacious staircase with enriched turned balusters. The 1967 survey noted that the upper two floors were empty and by 1970 it had become very dilapidated: the roof had gone, it was suffering from settlement and only the lino on the first floor was protecting the cafe below! The cost of a new roof and other repairs was estimated at between £4,500 [£18,000] and £5,500 [£22,000]. Nos. 34 and 36 were demolished in 1978.

No. 38–42: This was a Grade II late eighteenth century house on four floors with a symmetrical facade. The central entrance to the principal floor was reached by a fine flight of stone steps. The ground floor rooms contained some bolection-moulded panelling which may have derived from an earlier house, and there had once been a fernery on the second floor. The two late nineteenth century shop fronts comprised Nos. 38 and 42, the house above being No. 40. In the 1967 survey the entire building was found to be unoccupied and by 1970 the interior had become very dilapidated. The cost of repair was estimated at £10–12,000 [£40–48,000]. The house was demolished in 1978.

The site had long been subject to an outline planning permission for an extensive and comprehensive redevelopment scheme, which would have included an hotel, cinema and offices. But no action had yet taken place and the buildings had for years become increasingly derelict, with an inevitably damaging and depressing effect on other neighbouring property. By 1971 No. 30 had reached the stage when it had to be demolished. In the following year the site changed hands. The new owner wished to revise the application, and this gave the planning authority the opportunity to negotiate. The consultant therefore recommended that any new scheme submitted should incorporate the three most important frontages as an essential element of the design.

However, their condition was deteriorating rapidly. Another examination of Nos. 32 to 42 was carried out in August 1973 and, although No. 32 was found to be still structurally sound, Nos. 34–36 and 38–42 were in a bad structural condition. The survey observed that 'all floors and ceilings of 38 and 42 are in a semi-collapsed state while the third floor of Nos. 34 and 36 is collapsing, the fourth floor attics of both buildings being very dangerous'.

The new scheme was submitted in October 1973, after which various meetings were held and useful comments

Plate 41a Nos. 26–42 Lower Bridge Street

Plate 41b The hotel scheme
Plate 41c The present situation

were received from local amenity societies. Minor alterations were made as a result of these, and the revised scheme was given planning permission (with very detailed conditions) in October 1974.

The scheme included shops at street and Row level with offices above. At its highest point the new building would be of six storeys, but stepped well back from the existing four-storey frontages. A scale model made by the developers was carefully tested in position on the Bridgegate Area model and the Planning Department were satisfied that the extra height would not be unduly damaging to the environment. A firm condition was made that the three important frontages were to be either repaired or rebuilt and a suitable brick used on the new frontage.

But a changing financial climate prevented all work from going ahead on this scheme and in May 1976 the owners became bankrupt. The firm appointed by the Receiver to manage the properties commissioned another structural report. Their surveyors recommended that the building had reached such an advanced state of dereliction that 34–36 should be demolished immediately and 38–42 should be shored up to prevent it collapsing onto the street.

Application was made in May 1977 for Listed Building Consent to demolish Nos. 34–36 and 38–42. The application was called in by the Secretary of State, who decided to conduct a Public Inquiry. The Inquiry was held in February 1978 but, before the Inspector was able to make his recommendations, the buildings had become so dangerous that the owner felt obliged to demolish the properties in the interests of public safety. All that remains of the nine properties are the shells of Nos. 26, 28 and 32. Many suggestions have been made for the site and some have reached an advanced stage. The City hopes to see a smaller scale of development than was previously envisaged, comprising individual shop units at street level, with offices or a suitably sized hotel.

4.11 Nos. 22–6 Lower Bridge Street

4.11.1 *Nos. 16–22 Lower Bridge Street (pl. 42a)*

Next to the 'Hotel Site' is a fine Grade II eighteenth century house built for John Williams of Bodelwyddan, Attorney-General for Chester and Flint. The two upper floors present a grand if simple classical facade onto Lower Bridge Street, enriching the streetscape by its contrast in scale to the buildings surrounding it. The ground floor projects forward and contains three shops – Nos. 16, 18 and 22 Lower Bridge Street, the house comprising No. 20.

The house is now used as an Oddfellows' Lodge and Club and in 1974, with the help of grant aid, the Lodge carried out a programme of repairs to the roof. The original scheme, estimated at about £2,000 [£3,500] was to have included the reinstatement of the fine oak panelling to the hall, but this had to be omitted because of the expense. The street elevation was given a face-lift for European Architectural Heritage Year with the help of a Section 10 Grant.

Year	S10	T/S	City	Total HBG	Other Grants	Owner	Total Costs	1979 Equiv.
1974	373	446	445	1,264		1,263	2,527	4,422

4.11.2 *No. 14 Lower Bridge Street*

Between the Oddfellows' Lodge and The Falcon public house is a Grade II eighteenth century house with its four-storey gable facing onto the street. Nos. 14 to 22 are listed

Plate 42a The Oddfellows' Hall

for group value. In 1975 a restaurant chain took over No. 14 and applied for aid towards its restoration and improvement.

Year	S10	T/S	City	Total HBG	Other Grants	Owner	Total Costs	1979 Equiv.
1976		698	698	1,396		16,789	18,185	*30,187*

4.11.3 *The Falcon (Nos. 6–10 Lower Bridge Street)**

The last building which we come to in Lower Bridge Street, The Falcon, is perhaps the most important. It is of considerable architectural interest and complexity and is sited at a strategic position at the entrance to the Action Area. The solutions which have been found for its restoration are applicable elsewhere and the details have therefore been set out in Case Study 5.10. An interim grant of £5,000 to cover the cost of emergency repairs was made whilst negotiations for establishing a Trust to undertake full repair work were in progress.

Year	S10	T/S	City	Total HBG	Other Grants	Owner	Total Costs	1979 Equiv.
1979	5,000			5,000			5,000	*5,000*

* On-going scheme.

4.12 Grosvenor Street, Bunce Street and Grosvenor Place

Grosvenor Street forms the north-west boundary of the Action Area, and, with its role as a primary distributor of the central area traffic, it effectively cuts the Area off from the City's historic core. Except for the Grosvenor Museum and a house designed by James Harrison in 1851–3, now used as a branch of the Trustee Savings Bank, the buildings on each side are of no great architectural value, and their use and condition are peripheral to the problems of the Action Area. Several of the properties have been inspected by the consultants over the past ten years, and two of those on the south side, Nos. 23 and 25, were found to be in poor condition. But no grant aid has been requested.

Grosvenor Street and Castle Street are joined by a narrow lane, Bunce Street. In the Development Plan prepared for Chester in the 1960s, Bunce Street was included in an area allocated for shopping use and in 1966 a compulsory purchase order was served on Nos. 3–9 to enable the area to be redeveloped. However, by the time they were acquired in 1968, attitudes had changed and in their 1971 report the consultants recommended instead that they be repaired. Their recommendation was confirmed in the 1976 Draft Chester District Local Plan and, when they have been renovated, two are to be let to council tenants and two to private tenants. This pleasant row of two-storey

Plate 43a The Falcon

Plate 43b Bunce Street

Plate 44a No. 24 Castle Street

Plate 44b Nos. 20–22 Castle Street

Plates 44c and 44d The north side of Castle Street looking west and east

Victorian cottages is therefore likely to be given a new lease of life by a private developer. The other houses in Bunce Street are being improved by their owners now that the threat of commercial redevelopment has been removed.

Off Bunce Street is Grosvenor Place, a short cul-de-sac of Victorian terrace housing which was to have been exploited as a service access for the original hotel development covering 26–42 Lower Bridge Street. When the hotel site is developed, the terrace is likely to benefit.

4.13 Castle Street

Castle Street connects Lower Bridge Street with the Castle. It contains many fine buildings dating from the seventeenth and eighteenth centuries, although the consultants noted in the 1968 report that many of them had been mutilated by change of use. One environmental improvement of the last ten years has been the exclusion of buses because the road was far too narrow for them.

Passing eastward along the north side, the first building is No. 24 (pl. 44a). This is a potentially attractive small house of some architectural pretensions, possibly designed by Thomas Harrison but marred by an inappropriate addition on the front. It is owned by the PSA but may eventually be sold as surplus to requirements. If a new use can be found, this might provide an opportunity to restore it to its proper architectural dignity.

4.13.1 Nos. 20–22 Castle Street*

The two houses between No. 24 and the entrance to Bunce Street are both listed. No. 22 dates from the late eighteenth to early nineteenth centuries and is Grade II, but No. 20 is about a hundred years older with a fine baluster staircase and panelling, and is Grade II*. Both houses back on to the Grosvenor Museum, which is the City's local history display centre, and as they are owned by the City Council, they have been utilised as additional display and storage areas. However, their use was limited because of their poor state of repair and in 1978 the City decided to carry out a major scheme of repair and restoration.

Inspection showed that urgent repairs were required to avoid immediate and serious deterioration, but it was impossible to diagnose all the problems without opening up the structure. The City therefore contributed £2,500 towards an investigatory survey by a consultant for emergency repairs to the roof and applied to the DOE for a grant.

Following the survey, a scheme was prepared by a local architect and a contract was placed which was due to be completed by the autumn of 1981 at a total cost of almost £200,000, of which £111,250 was for the repairs to the structure and fabric. The City applied to the DOE for a 50 per cent contribution towards the repair costs and, in May 1979, the DOE agreed to provide the money in three phases: £5,620 during the 1979–80 financial year and £25,000 in each of the next two years. The City has allocated £10,300 and £10,000 from its Conservation Fund for

Year	S10	T/S	City	Total HBG	Other Grants	Owner	Total Costs	1979 Equiv.
1978			1,250	1,250		1,250	2,500	3,250
1979	5,620			5,620		5,630	11,250	11,250
Total	5,620		1,250	6,870		6,880	13,750	14,500

* On-going scheme.

1980–81 and 1981–82 respectively, giving a total grant aid of £75,920 over the three year period.

On the other side of Bunce Street is the Golden Eagle public house (Grade II). It was originally the private residence of Humphrey Bell, Sheriff to the City in 1469; the front was rebuilt in the eighteenth century and the interior contains some fine timbering and panelling.

4.13.2 *No. 16 Castle Street*

Next door, No. 16 dates in part from the seventeenth century and is also Grade II. But it was extended to form a factory and now accommodates a wholesale book distributors. A grant has been made towards the improvement of the premises.

Year	S10	T/S	City	Total HBG	Other Grants	Owner	Total Costs	1979 Equiv.
1979		2,881	2,882	**5,763**		5,763	**11,526**	*11,526*

Between No. 16 and Ye Olde Kings Head on the corner of Lower Bridge Street, the houses have been demolished, exposing the derelict land behind the 'Hotel Site' (Nos. 26–42 Lower Bridge Street).

4.13.3 *Nos. 1–5 Castle Street*

On the opposite side, Nos. 1 to 9 form a continuous terrace which is listed as of group value. Nos. 1 and 3 date from the late seventeenth or early eighteenth century and were probably built as one. They are marred by the insertion of large plate-glass windows at street level and an unsightly fascia above. In 1974 the tenant purchased Nos. 1 and 3 from the County Council, although the ground floor is used as a shop, the upper floors are empty. The consultants have drawn up a scheme for improving the facade of No. 1. This would provide sash windows on the Lower Bridge Street elevation and improve the shop window to Castle Street so as to make it more in keeping with the building.

The consultants also produced a scheme for the restoration of Nos. 3 and 5. No. 5 is now owned by the City who are hoping to restore it to residential use. In 1978 a scheme was prepared by a potential purchaser and house improvement and Town Scheme grants were offered for rehabilitation and repair. But the sale was not completed, and the City is still hoping to find a purchaser who wishes to proceed with a similar scheme.

4.13.4 *Nos. 7 and 9 Castle Street*

Nos. 7 and 9 which are a pair of early nineteenth century houses, changed hands in 1978 and the new owner applied for aid to enable him to repair the roof which was leaking badly. The grant was awarded in February 1979 and the work completed the following month.

Year	S10	T/S	City	Total HBG	Other Grants	Owner	Total Costs	1979 Equiv.
1979		592	592	**1,184**		3,801	**4,985**	*4,985*

4.13.5 *Nos. 15 and 17 Castle Street*

It has already been noted that the Action Area contains several unsightly 'gap' sites which, despite the intensive work over the past ten years, still remain undeveloped. One exception is the new infill between Nos. 9 and 15 Castle Street, (designed by the consultants and supervised

Plates 45a and 45b Before and after views of the south side of Castle Street

by a local firm of architects) which forms part of the St Mary's housing site described in section 4.14. The new housing sympathetically reflects the scale and character of the surrounding buildings, particularly Nos. 15 and 17, the gabled seventeenth century houses next door.

Despite being listed for group value, Nos. 15–17 had by 1971 deteriorated to the state where the City was faced with purchasing them to prevent their impending demolition. Several of the original windows had been removed and merely planked up. The gables were still surmounted by four plain and two ball finials, but parts of the plinth, cornice and parapet were missing. Structural faults on the west side of the building were evidenced by cracked brickwork and extensive damp.

The houses were however purchased by a local Trust who in 1974 applied for a grant of £1,706 towards their repair and conversion to two floors of offices and two of flats. The work was to include renewing part of the ground floor, re-positioning the staircases, demolishing the rear outbuildings, re-building the rear of the property, inserting new windows and doors, and cleaning and re-pointing the front elevation. The two properties were linked to enable the work to comply with the fire requirements. The extent of the repair work was greater and more expensive than anticipated, and in June 1975 grant aid of £7,298 [£12,771] was agreed, representing 50 per cent of repair costs in connection with an overall contract sum of £16,191 [£28,334].

The owners requested further aid to enable them to complete the roof and rear wall and repaint the front. In May 1978 they applied for another £1,925, representing 50 per cent of repair costs in a new contract for £5,640 to cover completion of the outstanding items. The City would have preferred a more intensive programme and a higher standard of work – especially that of repointing the brickwork. They decided to limit further grant aid to a final contribution of £600, plus £600 from the DOE. This was accepted and the work was finished in May 1979.

Year	S10	T/S	City	Total HBG	Other Grants	Owner	Total Costs	1979 Equiv.
1975		1,311	1,311	2,622		2,622	5,244	9,177
1976		1,034	1,034	2,068		5,404	7,472	12,404
1977		750	750	1,500		1,500	3,000	4,440
1979		1,182	1,182	2,364		2,364	4,728	4,728
Total		4,277	4,277	8,554		11,890	20,444	30,749

4.13.6 No. 23 Castle Street

No. 23, which has group value with No. 25, boasts a good early eighteenth century front which is a remodelling of an earlier house, and because of this the City agreed to make the owner a loan of £1,500 as well as awarding a grant to enable her to repair the roof and facade.

Year	S10	T/S	City	Total HBG	Other Grants	Owner	Total Costs	1979 Equiv.
1978		1,160	1,160	2,320		2,202	4,522	5,879

4.13.7 No. 25 Castle Street

No. 25 holds a key position at the junction of Castle Street and St Mary's Hill. It appears to have evolved gradually between the late seventeenth and early eighteenth cen-

46

turies. And, although a room on the north-west corner was altered at one time – probably to accommodate one of Bridgegate's many public houses – it retains a fine staircase with 'barley-sugar' balusters, possibly from an earlier building, and good panelling in the main first-floor room.

At the time of the consultants' survey the building presented a chronic case of misuse – as a tyre depot by a local garage – and the structure was beginning to deteriorate badly. The owners were actively considering moving to more suitable accommodation on an industrial estate. The consultants recommended that the City should encourage them and acquire this building as soon as possible as a 'checkmate' against other and perhaps equally unsuitable uses. They also recommended City acquisition of the workshop alongside as part of the St Mary's housing site.

In 1972 the City and DOE agreed to grant aid emergency repairs and in 1973 the City purchased the building and workshop for £6,783. The Second Interim Report recommended that full repairs should be carried out as soon as possible and that conversion to offices might be considered, as the building did not really lend itself to residential use.

In view of their commitments to repairs to Gamul Place and Ye Olde Edgar, the Council was unable to undertake the repair of No. 25 at that time. It was therefore offered for sale. An inquiry by a private purchaser to use it as a dwelling unfortunately fell through, but several

Plate 46a The staircase to No. 25 Castle Street

Plates 47a and 47b Before and after views of 25 Castle Street and St Mary's housing

enquiries were made by firms interested in converting the premises into prestige offices. The highest of these bids was accepted by the Council in September 1974, but the purchaser was unable to conclude negotiations. The building was therefore re-advertised and finally, in February 1976, sold to a local Trust for £750, the workshop being retained as part of the St Mary's housing site.

The first phase of the scheme for converting No. 25 into offices involved extensive rebuilding of the rear wall, and the second included extensive refurbishment, including re-roofing, pointing, new dormers, gutters, etc. Phase two was completed in August 1978. The two phases cost £16,700. In November the Trust applied for help towards phase three, the external brickwork and internal conversion, estimated at an additional £11,016. This bought the cost to approximately £27,770, towards which a 50 per cent grant was made. Works not eligible for grant aid cost an additional £2,000. The Trust later informed the City that the cost had increased by a further £300 and asked if the grant could be increased accordingly. Fearing that the phased work might continue indefinitely, the City and DOE agreed to award a final grant. The final cost upon completion in October was £30,000. Again the City had hoped for a more concerted approach to the repair and conversion work, and they felt that the brickwork repointing had not been wholly consistent with the character of the building.

Year	S10	T/S	City	Total HBG	Other Grants	Owner	Total Costs	1979 Equiv.
1973		80	80	160		161	321	652
1977		952	952	1,904		1,655	3,559	5,267
1979		5,976	5,976	11,952		14,240	26,192	26,192
Total		7,008	7,008	14,016		16,056	30,072	32,111

4.14 The St Mary's Hill area

The area around St Mary's Hill is probably the most picturesque in the Action Area. The 1968 Report noted that 'the stepped pavement, cobbled textures and dramatic slopes and levels, together with adjoining St Mary's Church and its fine churchyard trees, combine to give Chester an extremely attractive and characterful element of townscape'.

One of the policies recommended throughout the reports on Chester has been to encourage the resurgence of residential life within the City Walls. The Bridgegate Area is separated from the main commercial area and has a potentially pleasant environment; it is therefore particularly suited to town living. Historically its attraction is evidenced by a surprisingly large number of major town houses; these and other lesser dwellings all testify to the former residential quality of the area. The consultants, the Conservation Section and local estate agents have received numerous enquiries about residential accommodation in the Study Area, and in the 1968 Report the consultants advocated new-build town housing on the backland south of Castle Street.

4.14.1 St Mary's Hill housing (pls. 45b, 47b and 50a)

The St Mary's Hill housing site includes several parcels of land including a piece occupied by the Salvation Army, who were planning to move elsewhere, St Mary's Infants' School, which was to be closed, and the tyre store adjoining St Mary's Hill. The consultants recommended that the City negotiate with the parties concerned to bring this land into

single ownership and make possible a small comprehensive housing scheme. A feasibility study was carried out and the proposal was shown to be practicable.

The future of St Mary's School then came under further review and the County Council decided to keep it open when staff and parents made a strong case for the school to continue. This was a great bonus for the communal life of the area and the housing scheme was re-planned. An exchange was negotiated whereby a narrow strip of school playground was given up for housing in place of some of the land behind the cottages in Gamul Place. This was then made into a garden available both for the use of local residents and for the schoolchildren, for whom some play equipment was subsequently provided.

After alternative accommodation had been found for the Salvation Army, their site and that of the tyre store were purchased by the Council for £27,800 and advertised for development. When no offers were received, the Muir Group Housing Association Ltd came forward and acquired the land for a lump-sum price of £32,500 plus a peppercorn rent. A condition of the sale was that the development should follow the consultants' approved sketch design. Its detailed execution was placed in the hands of a local firm of architects.

The resulting accommodation comprises four town houses and garages on St Mary's Hill; two maisonettes and three flats on Castle Street; and three houses behind Castle Street. They have been made available for lease from the Housing Association, who received a grant from the City Council of £276,000 [£414,000] in 1976 to cover the costs of acquisition, construction and fees.

The work falls under the government housing cost limits with extra finance for 'site development'. Because the site is in a conservation area, an additional 'setting allowance' was made for sympathetic materials (eg brick and slates) and the more than usually complex roofs. A 'redevelopment allowance', together with ad-hoc allocations for foundations, was also available because redevelopment of a built-up site was involved.

4.14.2 St. Mary's Hill/Shipgate Street improvements

Not far from the St Mary's housing development is St Mary's Hill. Here the cobbled surfaces of the hill itself and around the corner in Shipgate Street have been repaired. But the reclamation of the cobbles underneath the tarmac at the top of the hill and in Castle Street has not yet been achieved. After prolonged negotiations between the City and the County, paved access has now been provided from Shipgate Street to Castle Drive and the City Walls, using grant money from the DOE.

Year	S10	T/S	City	Total HBG	Other Grants	Owner	Total Costs	1979 Equiv.
1978	3,000			3,000		6,000	9,000	11,700

4.14.3 St Mary's Rectory (pl. 13a)

At the top of St Mary's Hill stands the Old Rectory to the church of St Mary-on-the-Hill. It is an attractive Grade II building and has important group value with the church. Its street facade was evidently remodelled with gables in the mid-nineteenth century but on the garden side it retains its fine eighteenth century bay window and segmental sashes. The Rectory was purchased by the County Council in 1968; a minimum amount of conversion work was done without destroying good interior features, and the building

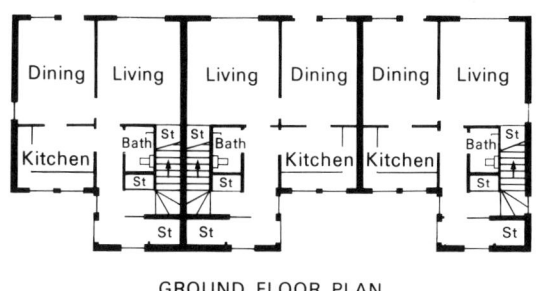

GROUND FLOOR PLAN

FIRST FLOOR PLAN

HOUSES AT THE REAR OF CASTLE STREET

FLATS AND HOUSES
ON CASTLE STREET

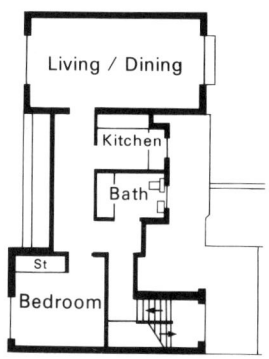

THIRD FLOOR PLAN

HOUSES ON ST. MARY'S HILL

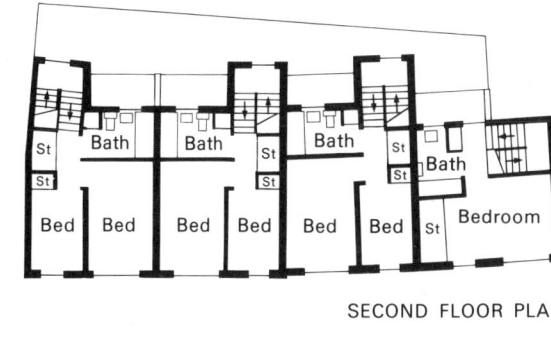

SECOND FLOOR PLAN

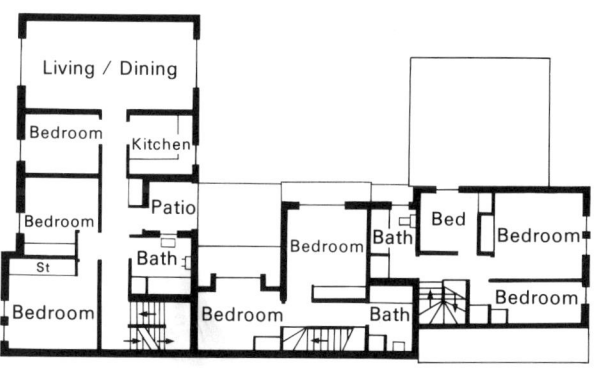

SECOND FLOOR PLAN

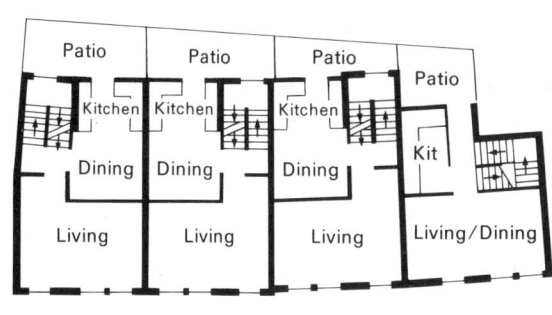

FIRST FLOOR PLAN

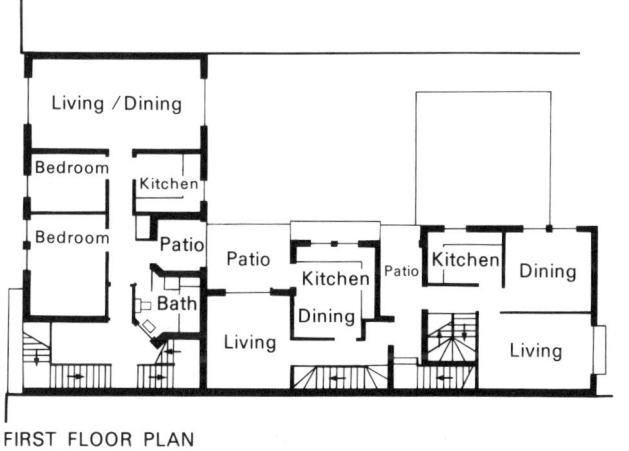

FIRST FLOOR PLAN

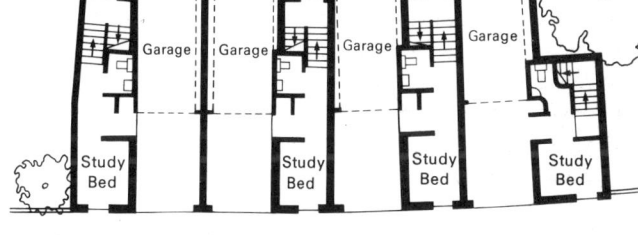

GROUND FLOOR PLAN

Metres

0   10   20

49

is now used as offices by the County Council's Education Department.

4.14.4 *St Mary-on-the-Hill, an Urban Studies Centre*

Opposite the Old Rectory is St Mary-on-the-Hill, a dramatically situated church which has been converted by the County Council into an Urban Studies Centre and is the subject of Case Study 5.6.

Year	S10	T/S	City	Total HBG	Other Grants	Owner	Total Costs	1979 Equiv.
1977	20,250			20,250		20,200[1]	40,450	59,866
1978	1,909			1,909	2,640[2]	12,364	16,913	21,987
1979	385			385		1,155	1,540	1,540
Total	22,544			22,544	2,640	33,719	58,903	83,393

1. Including £10,500 acquisition cost
2. Manpower Services Commission Grant

Plate 50a St Mary's housing from Gamul Place garden

Plate 50b (*below*) Looking down St Mary's Hill

Plate 51a (*right*) St Mary-on-the-Hill

TABLE No. 3   Cumulative total of investment: actual amounts
No totals are given for these investments because they were made at different times.   Table No. 4 gives the equivalent 1979 values of the individual and total sums invested.

Property	S10	T/S & S4	City	Total HBG	Other grants	Owner	Total Costs
St Michael's Church	16,000		9,195	**25,195**	7,413	12,971	**45,579**
No. 9 Lower Bridge Street		5,092	5,092	**10,184**		63,577	**73,761**
No. 11		1,783	1,783	**3,566**		6,174	**9,740**
No. 17		500	500	**1,000**		1,000	**2,000**
Nos. 29–31 (Tudor House)	105	4,737	4,842	**9,684**		19,255	**28,939**
No. 49		31	31	**62**		62	**124**
No. 51		769	769	**1,538**		1,538	**3,076**
No. 53*	375		375	**750**			**750**
St Olave's Church	5,000			**5,000**	750	2,861	**8,611**
No. 1 Bridge Place	30	272	272	**574**		575	**1,149**
No. 5		2,777	2,777	**5,554**		5,554	**11,108**
Nos. 7–9	63	214	214	**491**		492	**983**
No. 11		1,603	1,603	**3,206**		3,206	**6,412**
Bridge Place**	208		622	**830**		830	**1,660**
City Walls	1,500		385	**1,885**	1,155		**3,040**
No. 94 Lower Bridge Street*		34,892	16,000	**50,892**		26,761	**77,653**
Nos. 90–92	15,000	6,562	6,562	**28,124**		21,500	**49,624**
Nos. 86–88 (Olde Edgar)		19,250	11,395	**30,645**		30,990	**61,635**
Nos. 3–5 Shipgate Street	2,900			**2,900**		1,400	**4,300**
No. 12	767			**767**		767	**1,534**
No. 84 (Shipgate House)		6,000	6,000	**12,000**		54,795	**66,795**
Nos. 78–82 Lower Bridge Street	12,500			**12,500**		12,500	**25,000**
Nos. 70–76		1,748	1,748	**3,496**		8,118	**11,614**
Gamul House and Cottage and Nos. 12–13 Gamul Place }		35,600	38,468	**74,068**		12,568	**86,636**
Nos. 1–11 Gamul Place and Nos. 2–6 Gamul Terrace }					42,900	66,410	**109,310**
54–68 Lower Bridge Street*	7,864		7,864	**15,728**		37,972	**53,700**
Gamul Place Courtyard**	3,725			**3,725**	1,600	5,325	**10,650**
Gamul Place Garden**			750	**750**	1,000		**1,750**
No. 46 Lower Bridge Street		5,000	5,000	**10,000**		10,000	**20,000**
No. 44		2,300	2,300	**4,600**		5,234	**9,834**
Nos. 16–22	373	446	445	**1,264**		1,263	**2,527**
No. 14		698	698	**1,396**		16,789	**18,185**
Nos. 6–10 (The Falcon)*	5,000			**5,000**			**5,000**
Nos. 20–22 Castle Street*	5,620		1,250	**6,870**		6,880	**13,750**
No. 16		2,881	2,882	**5,763**		5,763	**11,526**
Nos. 7–9		592	592	**1,184**		3,801	**4,985**
Nos. 15–17		4,277	4,277	**8,554**		11,890	**20,444**
No. 23		1,160	1,160	**2,320**		2,202	**4,522**
No. 25		7,008	7,008	**14,016**		16,056	**30,072**
St Mary's Hill**	3,000			**3,000**		6,000	**9,000**
St Mary's Church	22,544			**22,544**	2,640	33,719	**58,903**

Notes
 * On-going scheme.
** Landscaping scheme.

TABLE No. 4 Cumulative total of investment: 1979 equivalents

Property	S10	T/S & S4	City	Total HBG	Other grants	Owner	Total Costs
St Michael's Church	28,000		16,091	**44,091**	12,973	22,699	**79,763**
No. 9 Lower Bridge Street		8,453	8,453	**16,906**		105,537	**122,443**
No. 11		3,120	3,120	**6,240**		10,805	**17,045**
No. 17		830	830	**1,660**		1,660	**3,320**
Nos. 29–31 (Tudor House)	105	8,290	8,395	**16,790**		33,316	**50,106**
No. 49		89	89	**178**		179	**357**
No. 51		1,346	1,346	**2,692**		2,691	**5,383**
No. 53*	375		375	**750**			**750**
St Olave's Church	8,750			**8,750**	1,313	5,006	**15,069**
No 1 Bridge Place	53	476	476	**1,005**		1,006	**2,011**
No. 5		4,610	4,610	**9,220**		9,219	**18,439**
Nos. 7–9	110	374	374	**858**		862	**1,720**
No. 11		1,603	1,603	**3,206**		3,206	**6,412**
Bridge Place**	308		921	**1,229**		1,228	**2,457**
City Walls	1,950		1,109	**3,059**	3,326		**6,385**
No. 94 Lower Bridge Street*		37,849	17,478	**55,327**		31,460	**86,787**
Nos. 90–92	19,500	8,530	8,530	**36,560**		29,571	**66,131**
Nos. 86–88 (Olde Edgar)		25,025	14,814	**39,839**		40,286	**80,125**
Nos. 3–5 Shipgate Street	2,900			**2,900**		1,400	**4,300**
No. 12	767			**767**		767	**1,534**
No. 84 (Shipgate House)		13,664	13,664	**27,328**		102,219	**129,547**
Nos. 78–82 Lower Bridge Street	12,500			**12,500**		12,500	**25,000**
Nos. 70–76		3,098	3,098	**6,196**		14,285	**20,481**
Gamul House and Cottage and Nos. 12–13 Gamul Place		61,456	67,278	**128,734**		22,797	**151,531**
Nos. 1–11 Gamul Place and Nos. 2–6 Gamul Terrace					75,075	116,218	**191,293**
56–78 Lower Bridge Street*	7,864		7,864	**15,728**		37,972	**53,700**
Gamul Place Courtyard**	6,519			**6,519**	2,656	9,175	**18,350**
Gamul Place Garden**			1,313	**1,313**	1,750		**3,063**
No. 46 Lower Bridge Street		8,390	8,390	**16,780**		16,780	**33,560**
No. 44		4,669	4,669	**9,338**		10,625	**19,963**
Nos. 16–22	653	781	778	**2,212**		2,210	**4,422**
No. 14		1,159	1,159	**2,318**		27,869	**30,187**
Nos. 6–10 (The Falcon)*	5,000			**5,000**			**5,000**
Nos. 20–22 Castle Street*	5,620		1,625	**7,245**		7,255	**14,500**
No. 16		2,881	2,882	**5,763**		5,763	**11,526**
Nos. 7–9		592	592	**1,184**		3,801	**4,985**
Nos. 15–17		6,302	6,302	**12,604**		18,145	**30,749**
No. 23		1,508	1,508	**3,016**		2,863	**5,879**
No. 25		7,547	7,547	**15,094**		17,017	**32,111**
St Mary's Hill**	3,900			**3,900**		7,800	**11,700**
St Mary's Church	32,837			**32,837**	3,432	47,124	**83,393**
Total (41 Schemes) at 1979 prices	137,711	212,642	217,283	**567,636**	100,525	783,316	**1,451,477**

Notes

* On-going scheme.

** Landscaping scheme.

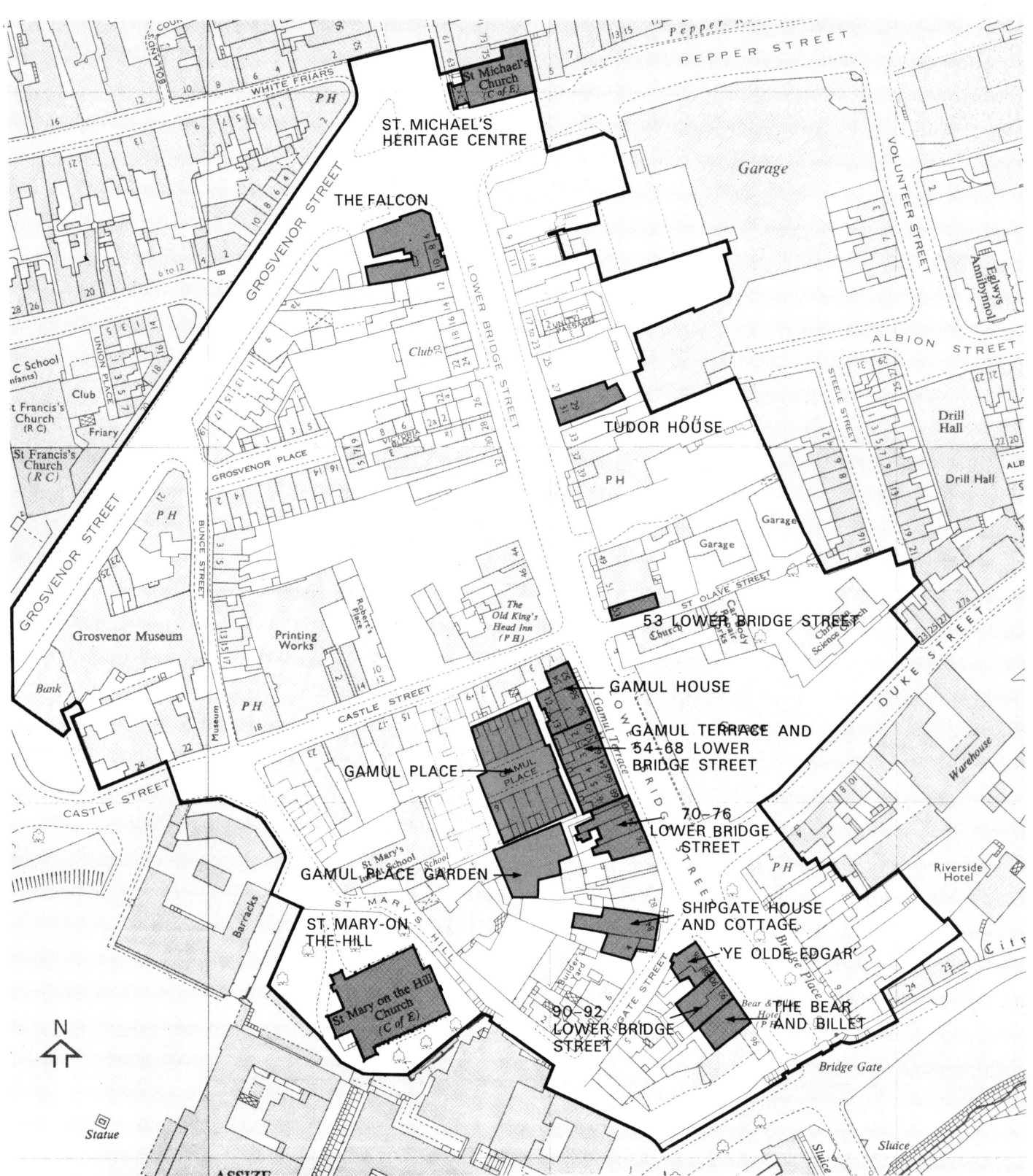

MAP No. 6 Case Studies

5 Individual case studies

5.1 The Chester Heritage Centre

A Heritage Centre created out of a redundant church

Following a suggestion from Lord Sandford (then Minister responsible for conservation) on a visit to Chester, the City decided to develop the idea of an 'Architectural Interpretation Centre' to encourage public participation and co-ordinate visitor interest in Chester's history and conservation programme.   Lord Sandford convened a meeting at which it was proposed that two redundant churches in Chester might be developed respectively as an Urban Studies Centre for students and an Interpretation Centre for visitors.   The former is housed in St Mary's Church, to the south-west of Bridgegate (see Section 5.6); the latter in St Michael's at the opposite corner of the Action Area.

St Michael's Church stands at the lower end of Bridge Street and is entered at Rows level.   Although on the site of the Roman South Gate, it is actually very near the heart of the historic city centre.   The church was declared redundant in 1972, becoming available just in time to be purchased by the City for £10,500, [£30,240] rapidly converted, and then re-opened in June 1975 by the Duke of Gloucester as part of the activities connected with European Architectural Heritage Year.

The oldest part of St Michael's Church dates from the fifteenth century, including a richly carved chancel roof of 1496.   It was mostly rebuilt in 1850 by James Harrison and the tower now forms an important landmark in the townscape of Bridge Street.   Very limited funds were available, but the exterior had already been vastly improved in appearance by stonework cleaning, paid for under the Special Environmental Assistance Scheme ('Operation Eyesore') in 1972.   Essential structural repairs were first carried out, and then designs were prepared by the City's Conservation Section and the consultants.   Models of alternative layouts were made.   The scheme selected was carried out by two local contractors and entailed removing disused Church fittings, adding a draught lobby and bookstall at the entrance and screening off the old chancel as a lecture theatre for audio-visual presentations.   The nave forms the setting for display screens, which were kept independent of the original structure and conceived rather as freestanding furniture, so that the roof and main structure are untouched.

Ideas for the audio-visual display were developed in discussion with specialists; preparation entailed a crash-programme of furious activity around the clock by the City's officers and the consultant team.   The twin-projector idea used in many earlier presentations was expanded to a 20-minute production of very high quality, with over 400 pictures back-projected onto triple screens.   This involved the use of six coupled carousel projectors with automatic fade-change and synchronised music and commentary.   Together with the exhibition, the presentation demonstrates vividly how much the present owes to the past and introduces Chester's philosophy of living urban conservation.   Commencing with a short historical survey, the exhibition describes the City's conservation problems and programme and shows in detail the way in which this has been financed, concluding with illustrations of conservation projects recently completed, especially in the

Plate 55a The entrance to Chester Heritage Centre

Plate 55b Location map

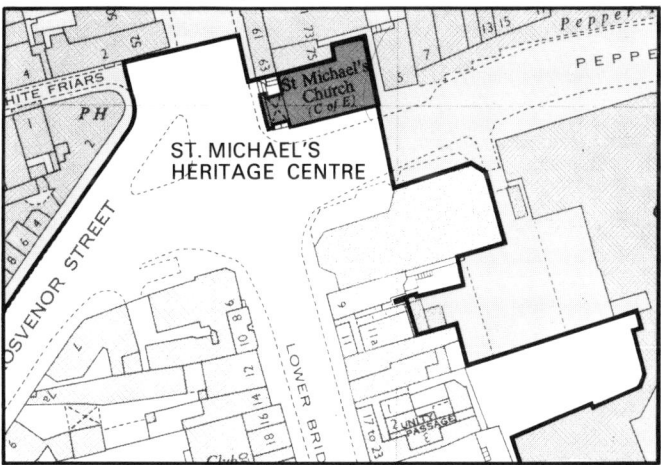

adjacent Bridgegate area. A planning model of the area has formed a central feature of this display.

In the first five years the Centre attracted over 20,000 visitors including foreign tourists, local residents and school parties, and it has been enthusiastically received. It has been useful for conferences and as a base for guided 'Heritage Walks', and is beginning to serve as a useful focus for sounding out views on planning issues by means of exhibitions and discussions. For example, in the spring of 1980, the Centre housed a seminar and exhibition illustrating a problem common to the centres of many of our historic towns – the proliferation of empty and decaying upper floors. It was possible to provide lectures, an extensive display of photographs and drawings and a superb half-hour audio-visual presentation to explain the problem and show possible solutions. Such a facility is a continuing asset; in the words of the Civic Trust News, 'Chester's Heritage Centre certainly fulfils its stated objectives: no visitor can leave unimpressed by the City's efforts. The underlying message is clear – if it can be done in Chester, it can be done elsewhere...'

5.2 Tudor House (Nos. 29–31 Lower Bridge Street)

Loans as well as grants by the City have enabled the restoration of one of the finest 'black and white' houses in Chester.

Tudor House dates from the sixteenth century and like most of the City's buildings, it has been adapted by successive generations: initially the first-floor Row was

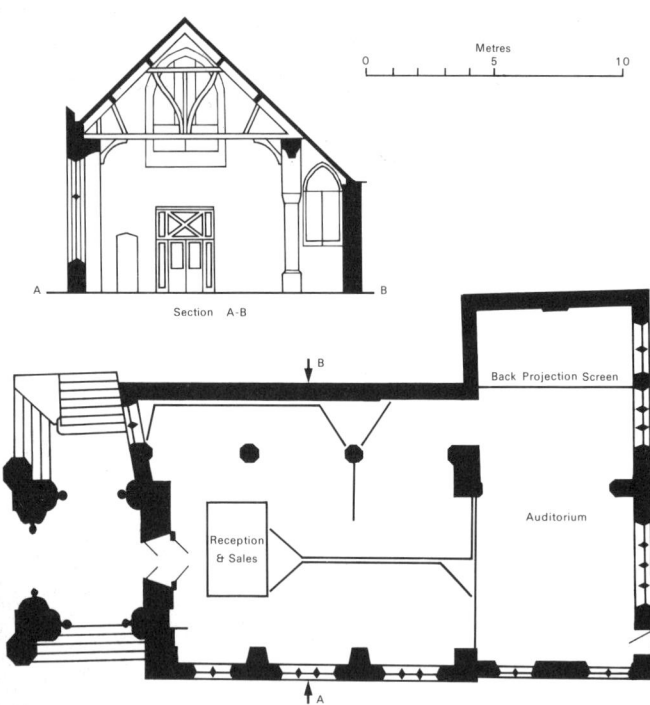

Plate 56a Plan and section

Plate 56b The Heritage Centre after cleaning

Plate 56c The exhibition space

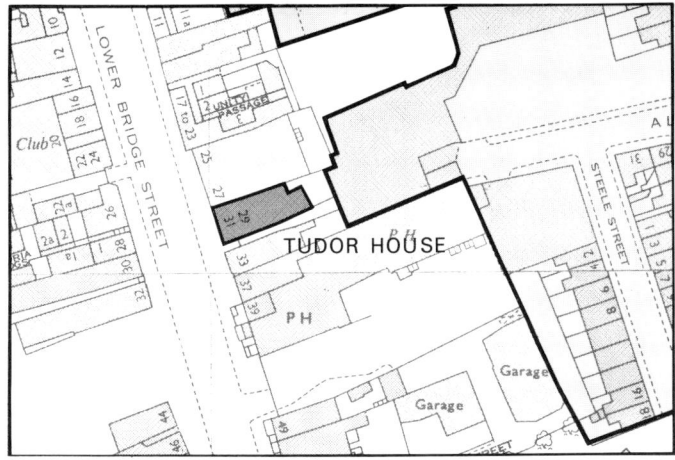

Plate 57a Location map

enclosed to form an extra room, then the two lower floors were given an eighteenth century facade, resulting in a curious impression that a Georgian base carries an earlier upper floor! Most of the original structure, however, still exists.

Towards the end of 1972 the owner commissioned the Insall consultancy to undertake a thorough survey of the structure with a view to converting Tudor House into a centre for displaying and selling antique furniture. The survey revealed serious structural faults. Most of the joints at the ends of the great cross-beams had failed, so that the tall timber-framed side wall had by now deteriorated to such an extent that it was collapsing in upon itself. Much of the load was by now transferred on to a window, which was by no means qualified for its new responsibility. Flying shores had been inserted some years before to prop up the side wall from its neighbour, but these were now rotten and useless. The timbering of the front elevation had evidently then been given a false extension, with curious lop-eared results.

Opening-up revealed the timber framing to be in an appalling condition, some of the joints between main posts and beams being so decayed by wet rot and beetle attack that they had ceased to connect at all. At one moment, the surveyor was forced to replace removed floorboards rapidly, for it became apparent that they were doing much to hold the building together!

Work started in April 1973. The timbers from the south wall were each carefully numbered and recorded and all those taken down were salvaged and set aside, to be reinstated in their original positions.

The south wall proved to be about half a metre out of plumb within a height of seven and a half metres – and this distortion was expressed on the main facade of the building which had 'lozenged' accordingly. It was impossible to correct this; and to have provided a straight corner would anyway have destroyed the symmetry of the facade. It was therefore decided to accept the existing lean of the old south wall, but to hang this from new steelwork inside. As the building regulations do not cater sympathetically for walls to be built half a metre out of true, much constructive help was needed and received from the Building Inspectors. Behind the central vertical post the new steel-work transfers the loads safely down to first floor level to be distributed on to brick and stone walling below, thereby retaining the building's structural integrity. The back part of the wall was rebuilt vertically on the line of the new steel, but it proved impossible to retain some of the lower brickwork of the chimney stack, and this was rebuilt using

Plate 57b An early photograph of Tudor House

Plate 57c The repaired property
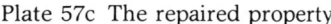

original bricks wherever possible. Some of the steelwork had to be welded in-situ and the local Fire Brigade was glad to 'stand-by' as a precautionary exercise.

Because it had been repaired in about 1965 the roof was at first thought to be in good condition. Unfortunately, it was found that a new roof structure had merely been laid upon the original defective timbers without first adequately repairing and strengthening them. The resultant increase in load was no doubt a factor in the subsequent collapse of the side wall. This problem could hardly be ignored. To cope with it and still provide headroom, cranked trusses were inserted to carry the purlins at mid-span. These tied the steelwork of the south wall across to the brick north wall, itself a reconstruction when a bank had been built next door. The main facade was thus greatly improved by removing the fake 'buttress' masking the old props and struts.

These additional works were beyond the owner's financial resources and he therefore applied for a loan of £7,220 [£14,656] from the City in addition to the grant. This was agreed by the Council in July but, because of personal problems, the owner was unable to accept the loan until May 1974. In the meantime, to permit the building work to continue, the City had to arrange to pay the contractor direct for the whole of the certifiable expenses in the hope of being recompensed at a later date.

By the time the second phase of the work was finished in late 1975 the City and the DOE had each paid out £4,737 [£8,290] in grants and the City was still owed the additional loan money. As a means of recouping the loan the Authority considered taking over Tudor House either as owner or as a mortgagee, but were reluctant to do so because of the problems of finding a suitable use for the building or alternative accommodation for the tenant.

Tudor House was eventually sold in December 1977 and the original owner was thus able to pay back the loan early the following year. In September 1978 the new owner applied for further grant aid for the repairs to the front elevation and internal repairs so that he could open up parts of the building to the public. In November the City and the DOE each agreed to contribute £175 [£228] towards the costs and by March 1979 the work was completed.

Plate 58b Window buckled under load

Plate 58a Plans of Tudor House

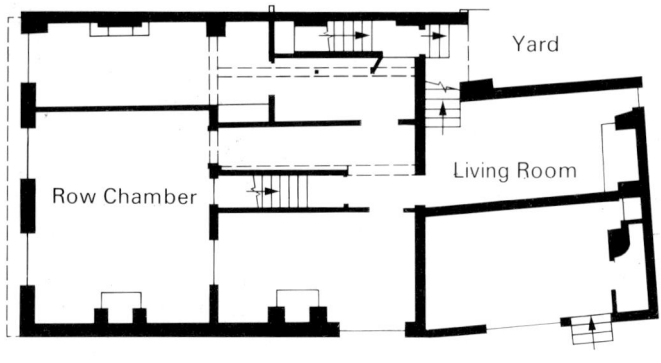

FIRST FLOOR PLAN

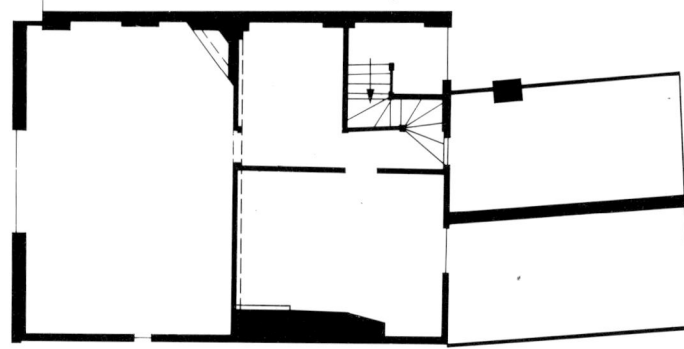

THIRD FLOOR PLAN

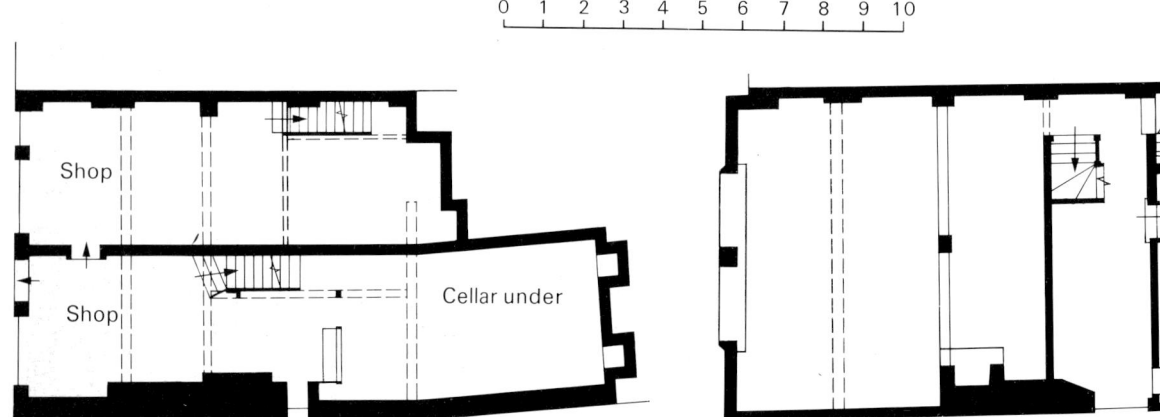

GROUND FLOOR PLAN

SECOND FLOOR PLAN

5.3 No. 53 Lower Bridge Street

Initiative by the City to prevent the possible destruction of an old cottage

No. 53 Lower Bridge Street is situated on the corner of St Olave's Street and has been built right up to the site boundaries on all four sides. An attractive little three-storeyed house dating from about 1700, it is of timber construction with a narrow gabled front facing onto Lower Bridge Street. It would appear at a cursory glance to be in reasonable condition.

The present owners, who purchased it in 1978, assumed that they would need to spend about £10,000 on repairs. They intended installing a snack-bar on the ground floor and living on the upper two floors.

They commenced work on it themselves at the beginning of 1979 but, because the problems seemed a little more complex than anticipated, they asked the City's conservation officer for advice in the hope of obtaining grant aid. However, upon looking at the building, he was extremely concerned about its apparent instability and he advised them that grant aid could not be provided unless they appointed an architect to carry out a detailed investigation.

The owners therefore appointed a local architect who after completing a detailed survey with the help of grant aid from the City and the DOE, estimated that a comprehensive traditional repair scheme would cost about £73,500 plus fees and VAT – over four times the original purchase price.

The structural integrity of the building had been completely destroyed because of mutilation over many years. The front wall was not tied back in any way, the half-timbered side wall was found to be only half-a-brick thick in places and leaning outwards, the floor timbers were completely inadequate in both section and construction, and none of the floors were adequately tied back to the walls. It was considered that the only way of retaining the present structure was to systematically replace and rebuild the various elements piece-meal.

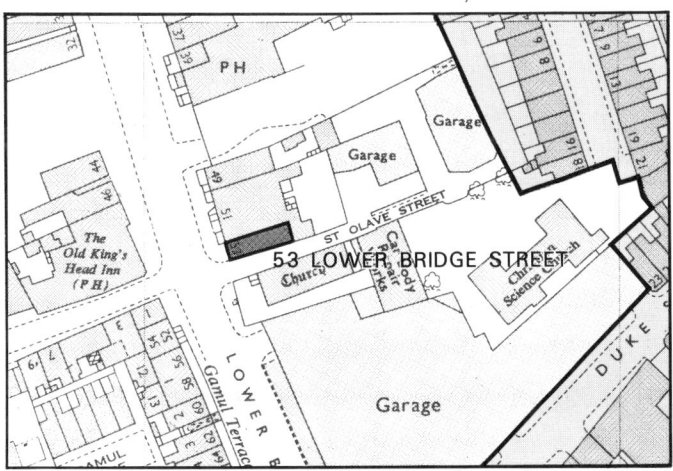

Plate 59a Location map

The cost of carrying out this work was of course far more than the restored value of the property – in fact the architect estimated that it would cost £20,000 less to demolish the existing building and construct a new one of the same floor area!

An alternative scheme was prepared involving the construction of a new internal wall running the length of the building from which the existing south wall could be hung. But even this scheme would cost £68,000.

The couple, who had had to move out and were in an extremely distressed state, therefore applied in November for an 80 per cent contribution totalling £54,000. But the City Council were reluctant to give a larger grant than 25 per cent because such a substantial amount would take too large a proportion of their available Fund and thereby deprive other applicants of assistance. This clearly would not solve matters, even if matched by a DOE contribution.

The City nonetheless realised that, if the scheme did not go ahead, the building would almost certainly have to be demolished and the construction of a new building would be unlikely because of the restricted nature of the site. Another gap would be formed on a key site opposite the entrance to Castle Street. The only way to prevent the demolition of No. 53 would therefore be for the Council to purchase it, restore it and either lease or rent it to the existing owners or others. Being exempt from VAT, about £10,000 would be saved. This procedure could only be justified if the building was of sufficient architectural or historical value. They have therefore asked the consultants to assess the intrinsic architectural quality of No. 53 as soon as finances are available to undertake the study. In their Conservation Fund programme, the City has allocated £15,000 for 1980–81 and £8,800 for 1981–82 in the hope that the DOE will agree to a similar contribution.

Plate 59b No. 53 Lower Bridge Street

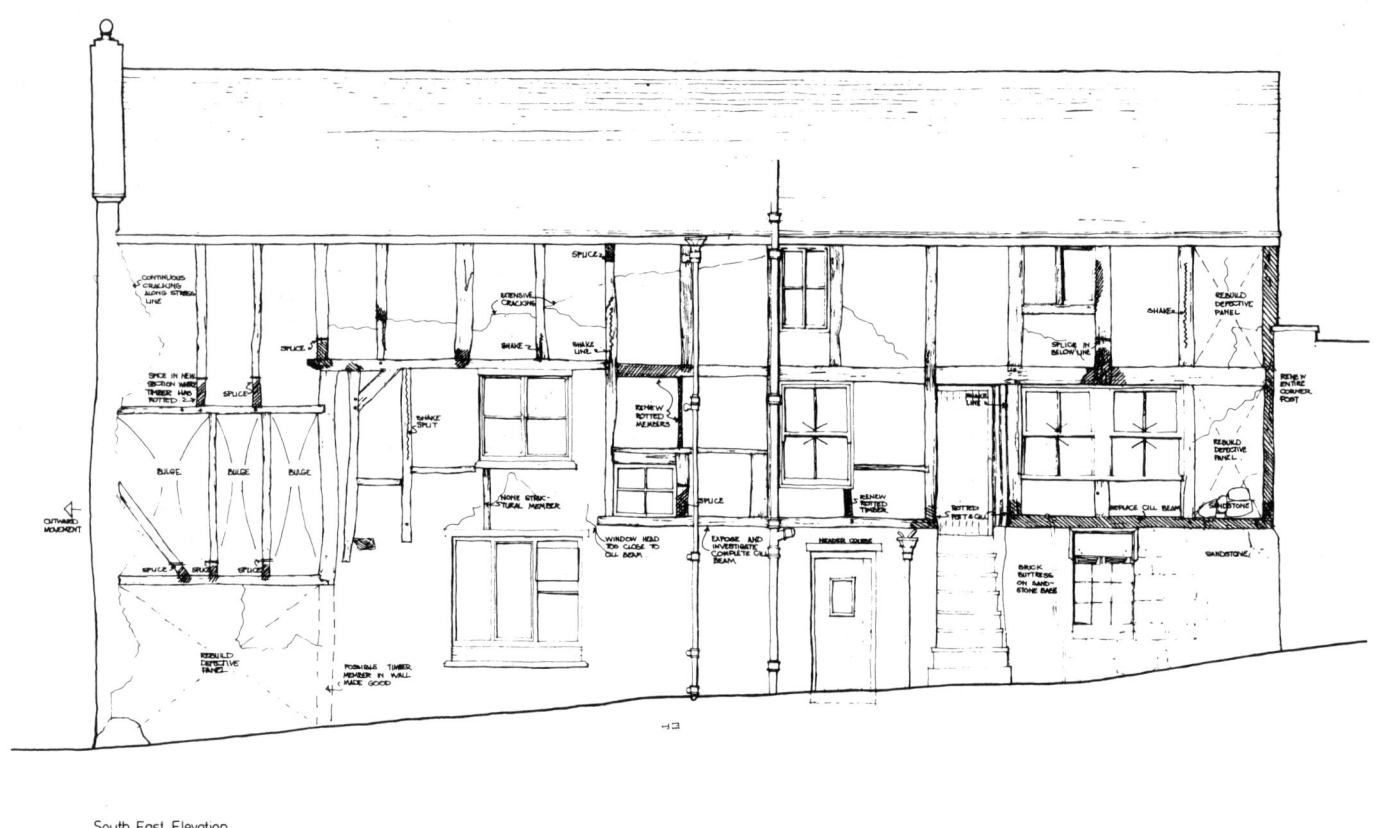

South East Elevation

Plates 60a and 60b Side elevation and plans of No. 53 Lower Bridge Street

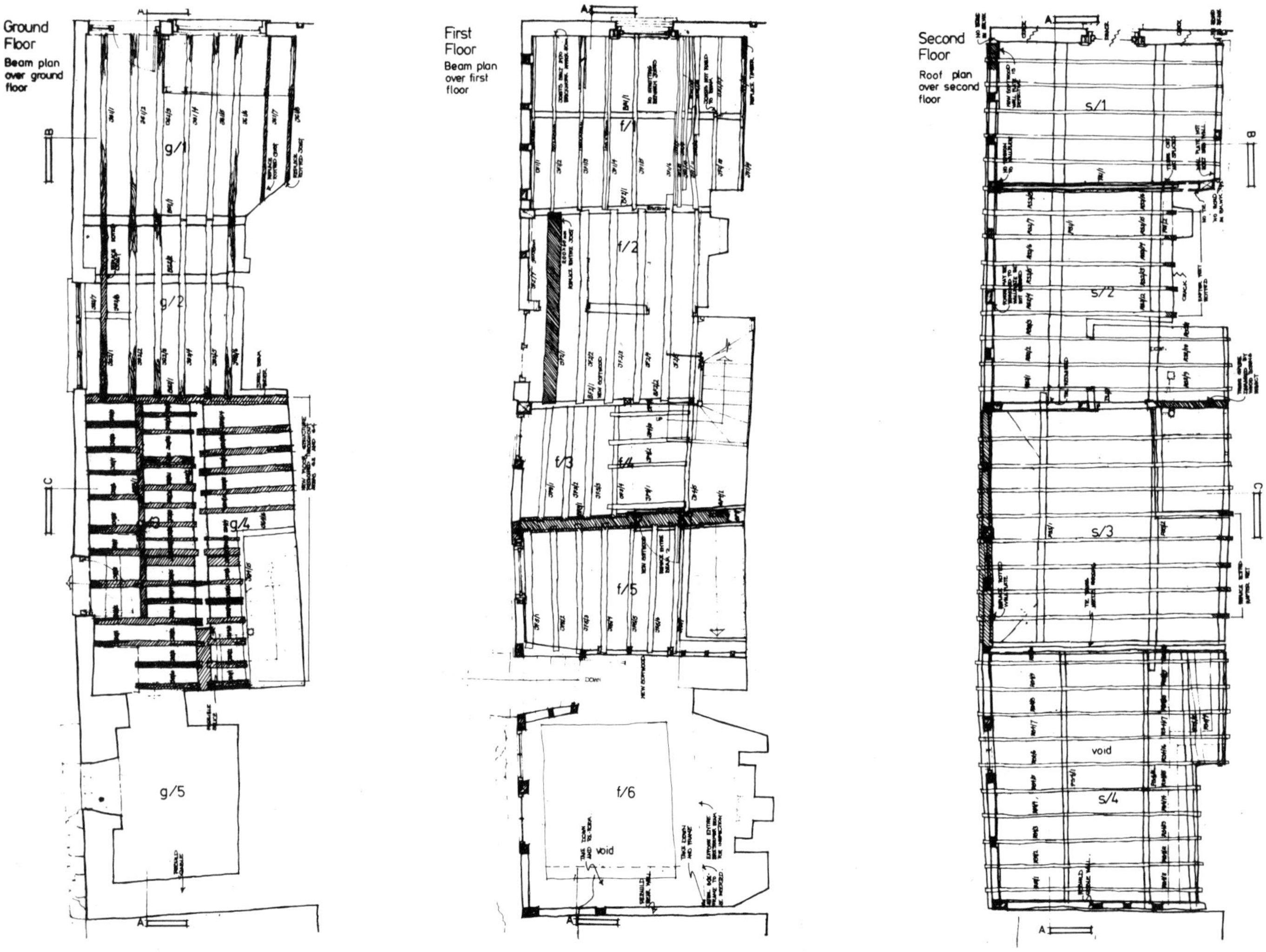

Ground Floor
Beam plan over ground floor

First Floor
Beam plan over first floor

Second Floor
Roof plan over second floor

5.4 The Bear and Billet (No. 94 Lower Bridge Street)

The problems of restoring a Grade I historic building in continuous commercial use

The Bear and Billet is a Grade I timber frame building with a particularly attractive seventeenth century facade. It was built by the Earls of Shrewsbury as the official residence of the Sergeant of the Bridgegate and was used for this purpose until it was purchased by the Corporation of Chester in 1666. It retained its original function for only four years before becoming a public house, which it has remained ever since. In 1752 and again in 1791 it was referred to as the 'Lower White Bear' and in 1809 as simply 'The White Bear'. In about 1857 this was changed to the 'Bridge Gate Tavern' and by 1880 to the 'Bear and Billet'.

For some time the pub has been owned by the small brewery firm of Quellyn Roberts and Co Ltd. During the early seventies, the front wall of the building and particularly the upper part of the gable (frequently a weak point in jettied construction) had been giving cause for concern. In October 1973 a meeting was held on site between the owner's architect, the City and the consultants to discuss the problem. Investigation of the upper floors showed that the beams carrying the front of the building were severely decayed by wet rot and beetle attack, and it was decided that a more detailed survey should be carried out immediately.

A full structural survey of the building was completed in January 1974. This revealed that the whole of the main front was becoming increasingly unsafe, the corner posts and main beams being rotten, and that the rear gable and flank walls were also in poor condition. Urgent restoration of the front wall was recommended, tying it more securely to the side walls and replacing any other defective timbers discovered during opening up. A second phase could tackle rebuilding. Necessary but less urgent items involved repairs to the roofs and chimneys, renewal of electrical circuits and redecoration.

The architects estimated that the work would cost over £50,000 [£87,500] and the City suggested that, because the owners were not able to pay the usual 50 per cent of the costs, the DOE might consider contributing half themselves and the City their usual 25 per cent, thereby halving the owner's contribution. Because the building was of national significance, the DOE agreed that a 50 per cent Section 4 grant rather than a 25 per cent Town Scheme contribution from the Department would be appropriate, but before they could make a precise offer there were a few problems to be overcome.

Plate 61b The Bear and Billet before restoration

Applicants for Historic Buildings Section 4 grants are normally expected to show that they cannot afford to undertake the work without financial assistance. This is particularly so in the case of a commercial organisation. The owner was therefore required to submit details of his turnover, capital reserves and accounts for the last two years. During 1975 the Company had had to repair another of their buildings which had been damaged by fire; this loss made a 50 per cent grant for the 'Bear and Billet' essential. But the Department felt that as the repairs would make tax relief available to the company, the DOE grant should be offset by this amount.

The next problem was therefore to calculate the amount of tax relief. This of course depends on the level of tax imposed, which in turn depends on the financial state of the firm. The firm's loss of profits from the fire meant that they were paying the lowest rate of Corporation Tax, 42 per cent. Tax relief would amount to £7,960 [£13,930].

Chester City Council had suggested a 50 per cent Section 4 grant to the DOE in February 1974, but it was not until April 1976 that the complications of eligibility and tax relief had been sorted out, by which time inflation had pushed the estimate up to at least £60,000 [£99,600]. The DOE therefore agreed to make a Section 4 grant of about £22,000]£36,520] – that is £30,000 [£49,800] less the probable tax relief. Quellyn Roberts took further advice and accepted the grant offer in January 1977.

Because of the outstanding quality of the 'Bear and Billet', the offer contained two special conditions. First, the architect appointed for the work must be approved by the DOE, and secondly, the building must be made accessible to the public. The latter condition is common to buildings receiving S.4 grants and is included to ensure that the general public benefit from the expenditure of public money.

The architects chosen were acceptable to the DOE because they had considerable experience in this kind of work. They were appointed in August 1977, and carried

Plate 61a Location map

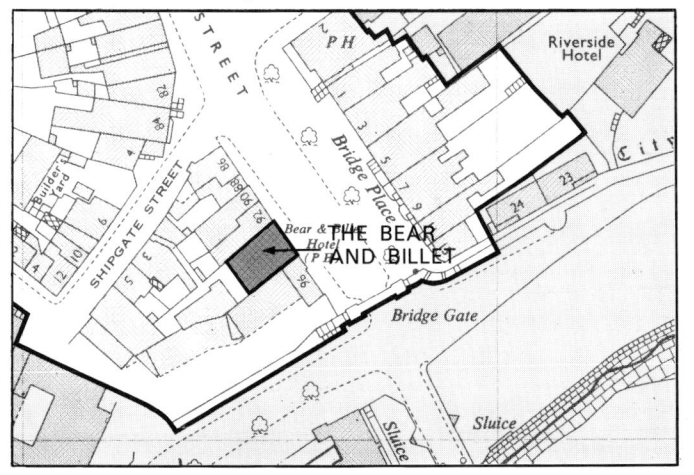

out an extremely detailed survey. Their report, estimate and proposals were submitted in February 1978.

Except for the rear gable wall, the whole building is timber framed, much of it in the original oak. It appeared that major repairs and alterations had been carried out between 1880 and 1890: tie bars had been inserted at each floor to restrain the front elevation, the main front tie beam had been strengthened with a second member, the roof had been renewed and several of the floors had received a second layer of boarding. As work proceeded, further opening-up revealed major problems. The roof was suffering from damp and lack of ventilation, the brickwork to the gable and chimneys required re-pointing, the timber to the front elevation needed detailed repair, and part of the timber framing to the south wall had been replaced by very inadequate brickwork. Because the pub was in use, the detailed internal repairs had to be done room-by-room.

The 1974 estimate had assumed that fairly drastic work was needed, including rebuilding the rear and flank walls, and inserting steel and concrete beams to support the floors. As the building had not been opened up at that time, the DOE had expressed doubts as to the need or desirability of such radical repairs. The more detailed inspection now confirmed their opinion, but other extensive repairs nevertheless forced up the costs.

As the work had to be done on a piece-meal basis and the amount of stripping and opening-up was largely conjectural, a day-work contract was agreed with a local contractor. This provided the right context for the approach adopted which was to disturb the original fabric as little as possible, so far as was commensurate with structural integrity. For example, work was programmed to proceed from the top down, so as not to disturb the critical state of the upper levels. On the side walls however, instead of replacing the heavy brick panels with light-weight construction, they were retained because they appeared to be part of the original construction and the missing parts of the timber framework were re-inserted.

Plate 62a Front facade of the Bear and Billet

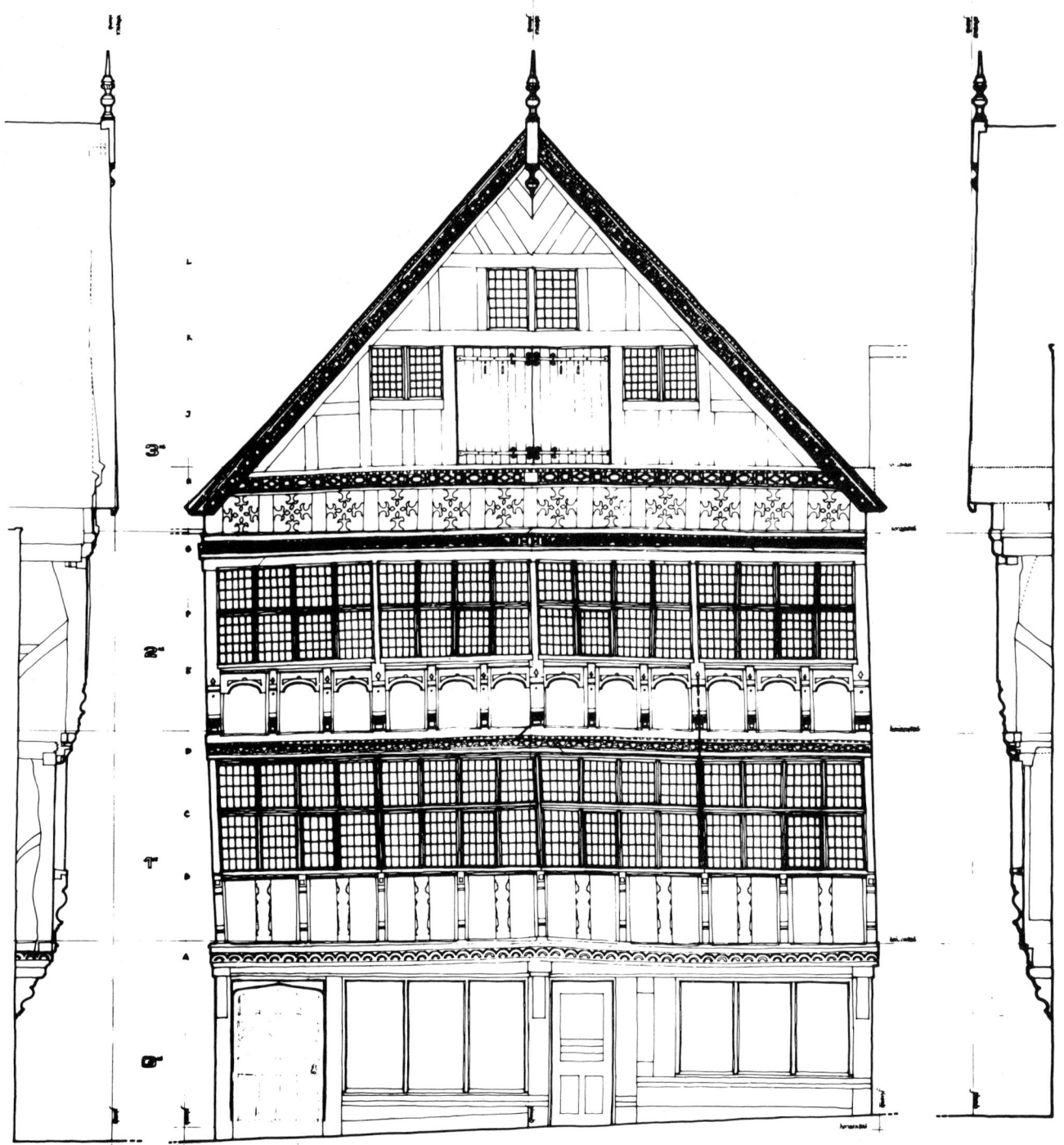

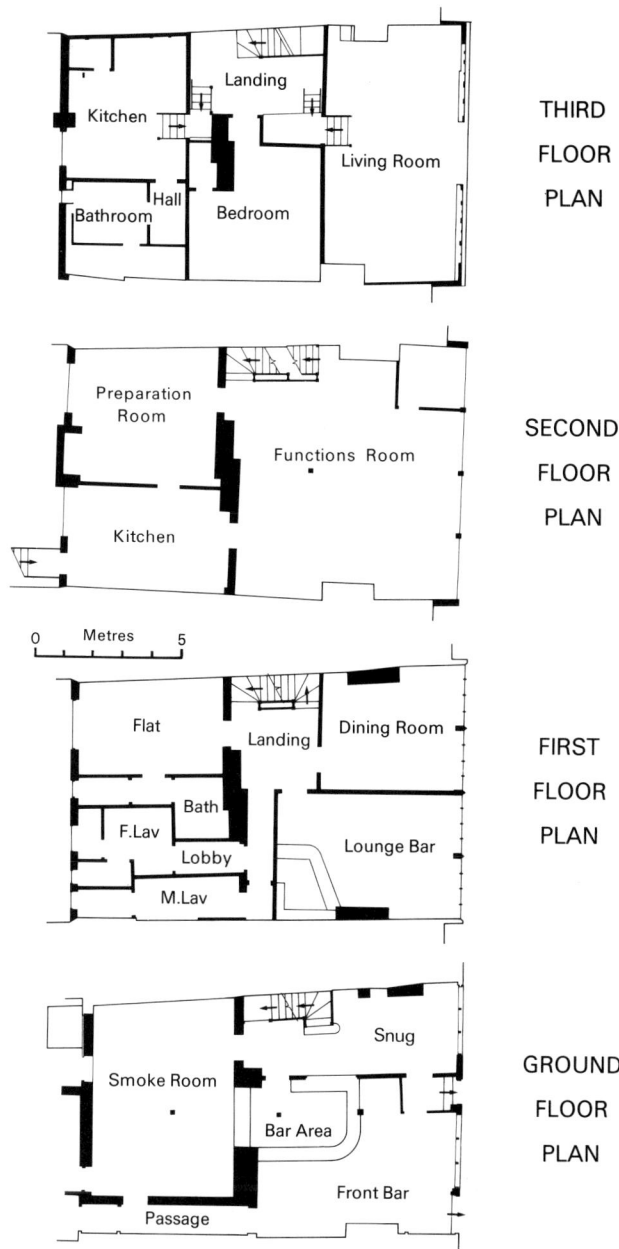

Plate 63a Plans of the Bear and Billet

THIRD
FLOOR
PLAN

SECOND
FLOOR
PLAN

FIRST
FLOOR
PLAN

GROUND
FLOOR
PLAN

Despite the problems of such a complex work of restoration in an occupied building, the contract was successfully completed in January 1980 at a total cost of about £103,000, including fees and VAT.

The question of access has been a bone of contention. The original requirement had been for 'adequate access by the public'. The DOE interpreted this as involving publicity on a national basis but the owners considered that as Chester is a major tourist centre, they were attracting quite enough people already. They wrote to explain that the Bear and Billet had been used as a Case Study by the Society for the Protection of Ancient Buildings, as a venue for international tours by British Heritage, and 'we even have them in droves through our own Crypt cellars'. The DOE persisted however, and made it clear that no grant would be available unless the owners agreed to wider public access.

The Department also sought to impose a new condition that the grant received would be returned if the owners sold the Bear and Billet within ten years. This was intended to ensure that the owner could not make a profit as a result of receiving a government grant, and also that, if new owners refused access, there would be no loss to the taxpayer. But it was subsequently decided that because the original grant offer did not include the ten year condition, it was perhaps unreasonable to insist on it at a later stage.

5.5 Ye Olde Edgar (Nos. 86–88 Lower Bridge Street)

A strategically-placed historic pub converted to residential use

The building known as Ye Olde Edgar is basically a good medieval and seventeenth century timber-framed building standing on the corner of Lower Bridge Street and Shipgate Street. Until 1884 it was used as a public house and in 1895 was converted into two separate dwellings. Although a considerable amount of the original oak framing was retained internally, the facade was extensively restored at the time of the conversion, making the apparently good condition of the exterior somewhat deceptive. For example, in the corner house rising damp had forced the tenants to retreat upstairs, abandoning the ground floor except for the kitchen. The owners were either unwilling or unable to undertake the necessary repairs themselves, and in 1971 the condition of the building was such that the consultants recommended to the City that they purchase it and put emergency work in hand without delay.

Negotiations with the owners were difficult to establish and no definite action had been taken by 1973, despite a good deal of shadow-boxing. Meanwhile the buildings continued to deteriorate, and a leaking roof uncomfortably sandwiched the tenants between damp penetrating from above and below. It became imperative for repairs to be carried out before the tenants despaired and before the Public Health Inspectors were forced to condemn the building. Therefore the City Council reluctantly resolved to use their statutory powers to ensure its safety. But before the notices were issued, the owner contacted the Council and the purchase was successfully negotiated.

Emergency damp-proofing works were immediately carried out and both tenants were found alternative accommodation in Council housing stock until their own homes could be made habitable again.

In 1976 a fully comprehensive scheme of repair and improvement including a proper fire-break between the two dwellings was prepared by the Insall consultancy; this provided a more logical division of the accommodation which had been interlocked in a most curious fashion. The repair work proved to be unusually taxing. Past alterations and decay in the oak framing had destroyed much of its

Plate 63b Location map

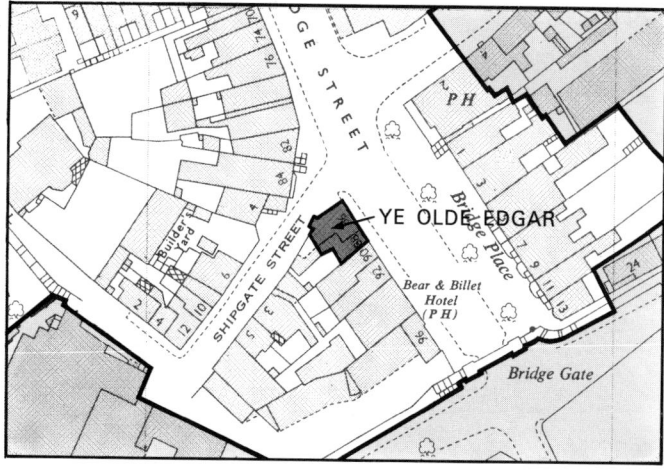

integrity, and the big central brick chimney was found to be supported perilously upon rotten timbers. These were cautiously replaced with steel joists, but elsewhere the framing timbers were carefully repaired with new oak.

Work started in June 1977 at an estimated cost of £57,700 [£85,396] of which £43,280 [£64,054] was for repair work eligible for grant aid. The scheme was completed in June 1978 and the tenants have now been reinstated.

Plate 64a Ye Olde Edgar: an early photograph

Plate 64b A recent view of the bottom of Lower Bridge Street, with Ye Olde Edgar on the right

5.6 St Mary-on-the-Hill

A redundant church becomes an Urban Studies Centre

The church of St Mary-on-the-Hill is a splendid mainly fifteenth and sixteenth century building of red Bunter sandstone built on the escarpment above the Old Dee Bridge – the original river crossing point. A church has stood on this spot since the twelfth century and the present building was extensively restored in about 1890. It contains several important monuments, fragments of medieval wall paintings and a superb decorated timber roof which was brought from Basingwerk Abbey, North Wales, in 1535.

An inspection in 1960 indicated that a great deal of the soft sandstone, which requires frequent restoration, now needed resurfacing. But by later 1975 very little work had been done and emergency repairs were needed to several of the mullions. By that time the church had been declared

Plate 65a St Mary-on-the-Hill

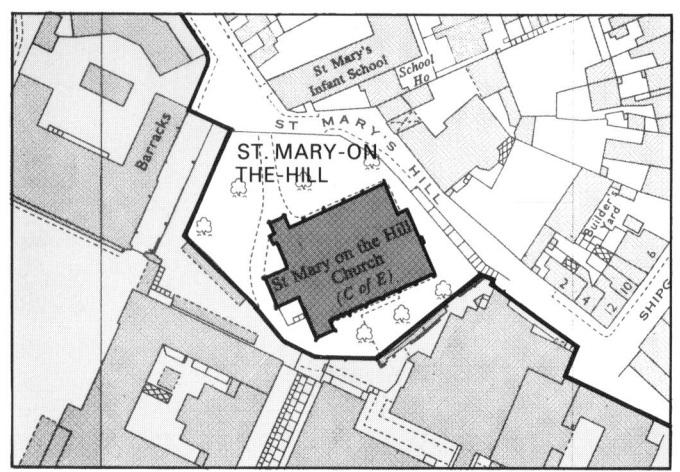

Plate 66a Location map

redundant and Cheshire County Council were negotiating with the church authorities to purchase it for £10,500 [£18,375] and convert it into an Urban Studies Centre.

The impetus for study centres came largely from a report to the United Nations Conference in 1972 by a Working Party chaired by the Countess of Dartmouth. In 1973, a Council for Urban Studies was set up by the Town and Country Planning Association, and the Royal Institute of British Architects promulgated the idea. The proposal for such a centre in Chester followed the meeting convened by Lord Sandford.

The work was divided into phases. The first involved essential work to the masonry, roof covering, rainwater goods and floors, and provision of such amenities as toilets, a warden's office, a kitchen and adequate heating and lighting. The second phase was devoted to restoring the monuments and the ceiling and carrying out various minor repairs.

The total cost of the first phase was estimated at £29,950 [£49,717] and in August 1976 the DOE agreed to a Section 10 grant of 50 per cent for both the work in phase one and the purchase price. The final cost of the phase was however £40,000 [£66,400].

In November 1976 the Council submitted their request for help on phase two, which was to cost £16,913 [£28,076]. A grant was forthcoming from the Manpower Services Commission towards the cost of restoring the particularly fine monuments. While not all of the work included in the second phase was eligible for grants under Section 10, the DOE agreed to provide a further small grant towards the cost of certain items of work.

Both phases have now been completed, including further aid towards improving the external paving, and the Centre was opened in June 1979. Besides a study space and library service for the Urban Studies project, there is information relating to urban areas and an exhibition space. These facilities enable it to be used both for architectural interpretation and as a general meeting place for County Council functions, and other purposes. With the help of Cheshire County Council, a valuable church has thus been saved and is being actively used for the further understanding of the environment and man's concentrated impact upon it.

Plates 66b and 66c The interior and the fine roof of St Mary's before conversion

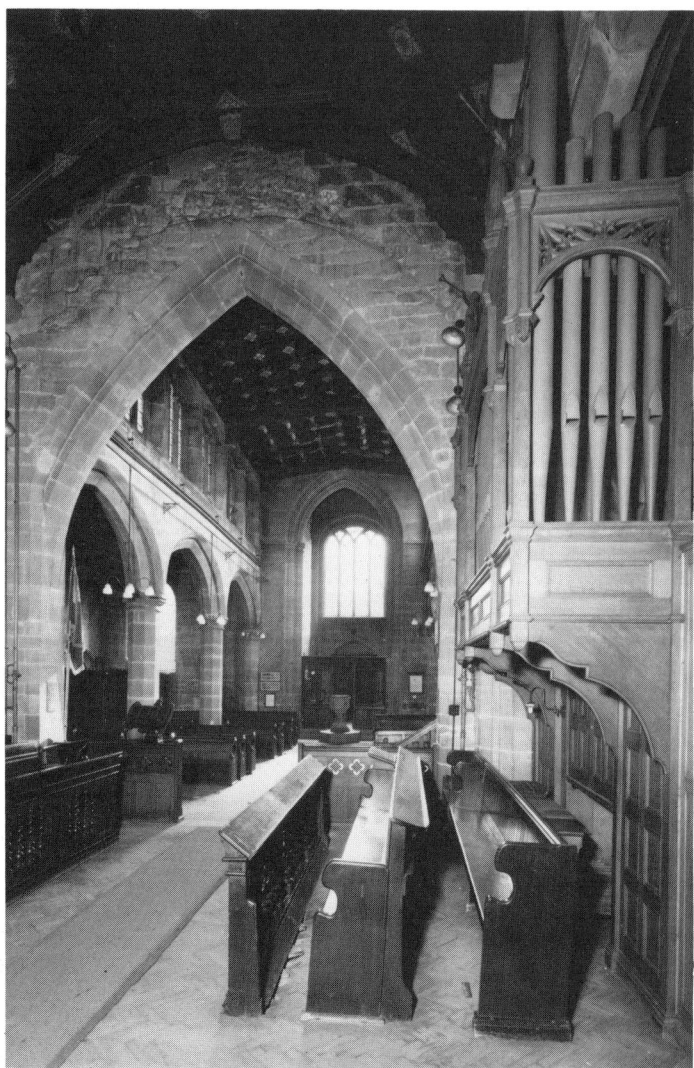

5.7 Shipgate House and Cottage (No. 84 Lower Bridge Street and No. 4 Shipgate Street)

The preservation of a pair of historic houses by the County

Shipgate House stands prominently at the corner of Lower Bridge Street and Shipgate Street, opposite Ye Olde Edgar. Listed Grade II, the house has an impressive facade with projecting cornice and an ornate doorcase. It is characteristic of Chester's buildings in containing elements of many dates; the undercroft is medieval, the rear section above basement level is basically a typical town house of about 1670–80 whilst the front is eighteenth century. It contains fine decorative plasterwork. Shipgate Cottage, alongside, also has an eighteenth century front; but repair work uncovered a medieval oak truss of about 1580 surviving from an earlier building. Shipgate House and the adjacent Cottage were purchased by the County Council at the end of 1963 for £24,500 [£113,435]. They intended eventually to pull it down to make way for the extension of County Hall to the west. Therefore, only sufficient emergency repairs were carried out to keep it habitable and no maintenance work was done for several years. It was occupied by an antique dealer, but he moved out in May 1968 and the building became unoccupied.

In the 1960's the County Council had been keen to proceed with demolition and redevelopment but, when the

Plate 67a Shipgate House; Shipgate Cottage is on the left

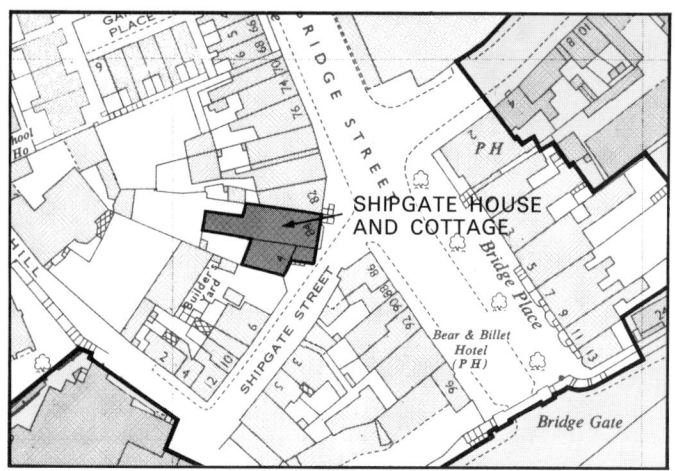

Plate 68a Location map

City made it clear that such an action would conflict with their conservation policy for the area, the County reviewed their earlier proposals. A detailed inspection in April 1969 revealed serious structural defects in the roof and rear wall and, with a view now to saving the building, the County appointed architects to prepare a report on the necessary first-aid repairs and on the longer term economic future of both the House and the Cottage.

The architects produced a scheme for converting the House into an annexe containing a staff recreation centre on the ground floor, self-contained flats on the first and second floors and commercial premises in the basement. The cost of phase one, repairing the buildings and making them structurally stable, was estimated at £12,500 [£55,750] and phase two, the conversion and renovation, a further £33,250 [£148,295]. The Council would then have 780 sq m of useable space. In July 1970 the County decided to proceed.

But before work started, the combined estimate had risen to over £60,000 [£211,200]. The County sought economies and work commenced on a revised scheme in June 1971. The initial emergency repairs took three months (phase one) and included stabilisation of the south wall, new brickwork and repairs to the staircase, roof covering and structure.

The work revealed that the rear of Shipgate House was in a worse condition than had been expected. Therefore it was decided that, while the front part of the House as far back as the staircase would be repaired and restored, the rear part should be taken down and rebuilt in modern construction. The final cost of phase one was £11,200 [£32,256] and the work received a 50 per cent Town Scheme grant from the City and the DOE.

Phase two commenced in October 1972. The final scheme retained the original recreational, commercial and residential uses but also included an exhibition space in the roof, where it was possible to preserve the original heavy oak truss and purlins. During the contract it was necessary to take down and rebuild some of the brickwork on the front because it had become dangerous, and to repair the pediment over the front door.

The final cost of phase two, which was finished in April 1974, was £55,600 [£97,300]. Of this, £25,000 [£43,750] was for repair work eligible for grant aid. However, instead of a combined DOE/City grant under the Town Scheme of £12,500 [£21,875], only £6,400 [£11,200] was offered. This covered that portion of the work which had not already commenced prior to application for grant being made. It was felt that a grant should not be offered for work already in hand or completed.

The front facade of the completed building now forms one of the most attractive sights on the approach to the town centre from the south. The rear garden has been landscaped and linked through to the adjoining St Mary's Rectory, also in County ownership.

Plates 68b and 68c The staircase and back of Shipgate House before restoration

Plates 69a and 69b Shipgate Cottage and its doorcase before restoration

Plate 69c The junction of Shipgate Street and Lower Bridge Street. Nos. 70–76 (Case Study No. 5.8) are on the right

5.8 Nos. 70–76 Lower Bridge Street

Using upper floors by linking through the party walls

Nos. 70 and 74 Lower Bridge Street once comprised a single eighteenth century brick building of four storeys (there being no No. 72), but they now have separate entrances and staircases and the dividing wall is hidden behind the central blind window. Only the roof space is continuous.

When inspected in 1971, both buildings were in use as ground floor shops, with multiple occupancy lock-up bedrooms above. Access to inspect No. 74 was not available, but No. 70 was noted as needing repair.

During 1972 the consultants were asked to prepare a scheme on the owner's behalf to convert the upper floors of No. 70 into a four-bedroom dwelling for himself and his family, but even with grant aid the scheme proved too expensive.

He therefore sold it to a local Trust, and in June 1973 their architects applied for grant aid to enable them to convert the upper floors to offices. Of the total cost of £4,720 [£9,582], £2,480 [£5,034] was eligible for aid and a 50 per cent Town Scheme (DOE/City) grant was offered.

However, in September the Trust submitted a further application for aid towards the restoration and conversion of No. 74 into offices and asked that both properties should be considered together. Structurally, both buildings were fairly sound but decoratively they were in bad shape. Repairs entailed strengthening the front wall at ground level, repointing brickwork and repairing the slate roof. Derelict buildings at the rear were also to be cleared to form a patio.

Work on the two properties started at the beginning of 1974. But by the summer the costs had risen from £7,788 [£13,629] to nearly £11,000 [£19,250] because of inflation, VAT and additional works, and the architects applied for further aid.

The reconstructed building provided 210 sq m of offices, including new toilet facilities, heating and lighting. The interiors were refurbished and joined through the party wall on two levels.

In 1973 the owners of No. 76 obtained a 50 per cent Town Scheme grant of £278 [£564] towards a new roof. Nos. 70 to 76 now form a series of linked offices and, together with the shops on the ground floor of Nos. 70 and 74, are fully occupied.

Plate 70a Location map

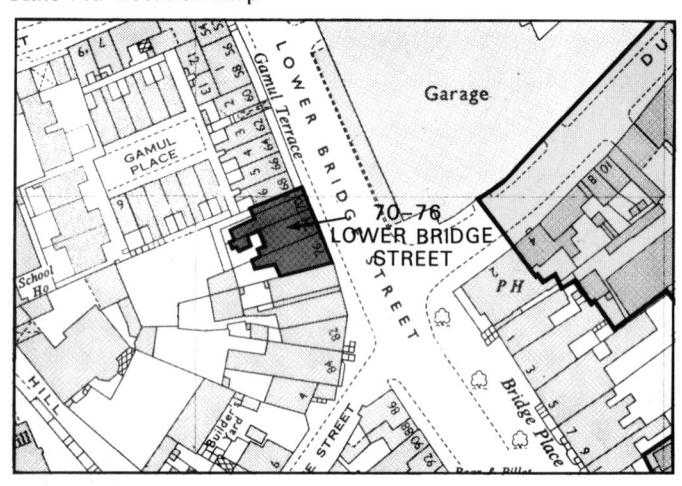

Plate 70b Plans of Nos. 70–74 Lower Bridge Street, linked through their party walls

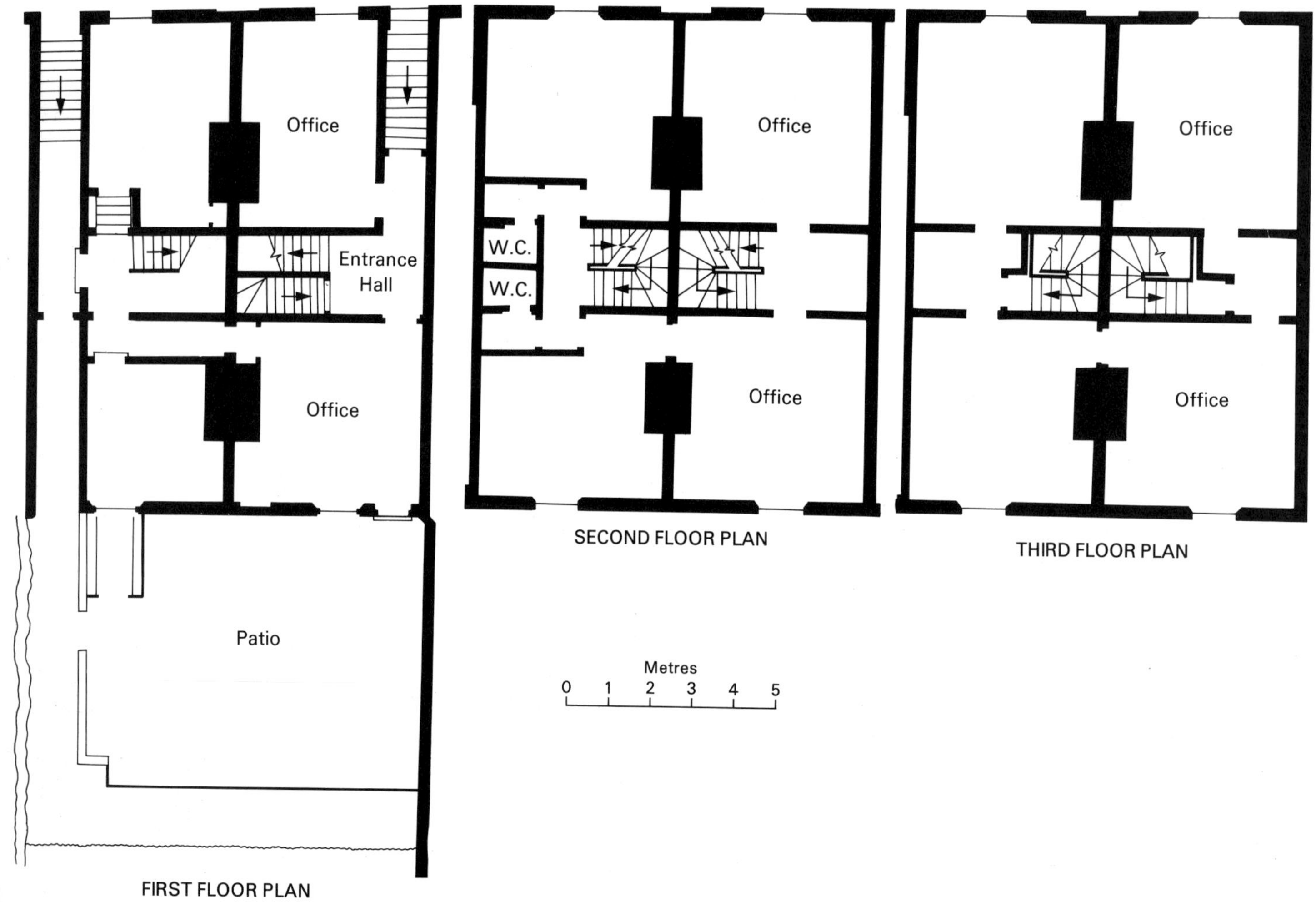

FIRST FLOOR PLAN

SECOND FLOOR PLAN

THIRD FLOOR PLAN

Metres
0 1 2 3 4 5

5.9 The Gamul House complex

The restoration and landscaping of both the street frontage and the backlands of a substantial part of the Action Area

Between No. 70 Lower Bridge Street and No. 1 Castle Street there is a complex of buildings named after Sir Francis Gamul, a merchant and Mayor of Chester in the seventeenth century. This comprises at the north end the former Gamul Cottage (No. 52 Lower Bridge Street) beside which a stairway on Lower Bridge Street leads up to a walkway alongside the street at first floor level. This gives access to Gamul Terrace, a building group consisting of Gamul House (No. 1) and five terrace houses (Nos. 2–6). No. 1 and the upper part of Gamul Cottage provide what is to all appearances a single building of very distinguished

Plates 71a and 71b The front of Gamul House before and after restoration

character. Beneath the raised pedestrian walkway and extending back under Gamul Terrace are eight shop units (Nos. 54–68 Lower Bridge Street). To the rear of Gamul House and Cottage is Gamul Place. This is a secluded court surrounded by thirteen small Victorian terrace properties and approached by a covered passageway between Nos. 60 and 62 Lower Bridge Street. The whole building group was in single ownership along with a small inaccessible area of land to the south of Gamul Place, and was acquired by the City as a single entity.

With the help of grant aid, this whole group has been considerably improved to form one of the most encouraging successes of the Action Area.

5.9.1 *Gamul House, Gamul Cottage and Nos. 12–13 Gamul Place*

Gamul House and Cottage form a single building listed as Grade II★ containing a good open Jacobean hall dating from about 1620. An etching of 1846 shows cast-iron windows by then inserted in the east wall; and these remain, but a curious tower shown projecting at the south end (see Plate 4a) has since been removed to provide access to Nos. 2–6 Gamul Terrace. Since the end of the last century, Gamul House has been used successively as an organ builder's workshop, an antiques showroom and an architect's office. The building formerly included a three-storey section to the north known as Gamul Cottage. At the rear are two cottages in Gamul Place, Nos. 12 and 13. A long period of structural neglect culminated in 1972 in the

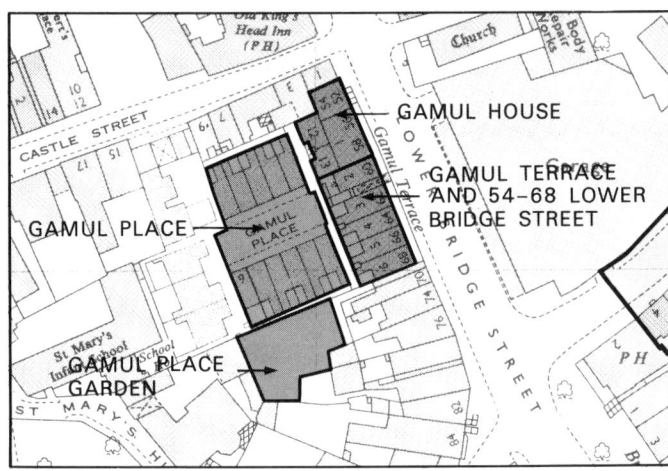

Plate 72a Location map

collapse of the hall roof and – despite emergency repairs – in the abandonment of the building. In an effort to save the property, the City purchased it the following year, installed emergency propping at a cost of about a thousand pounds and instructed Donald Insall to proceed with the repairs. At a time when many building firms were fully stretched, advertisements for tenders brought no response; so finally a negotiated contract was placed.

The original estimate, produced in 1972, was for £41,600 [£119,808] and the DOE had agreed to contribute £10,400 [£29,952] (25 per cent). But when the City purchased it later that year, the DOE agreed to foot half the bill

Plates 72b and 72c The main hall of Gamul House during and after restoration

Plate 73a Plans of the Gamul complex

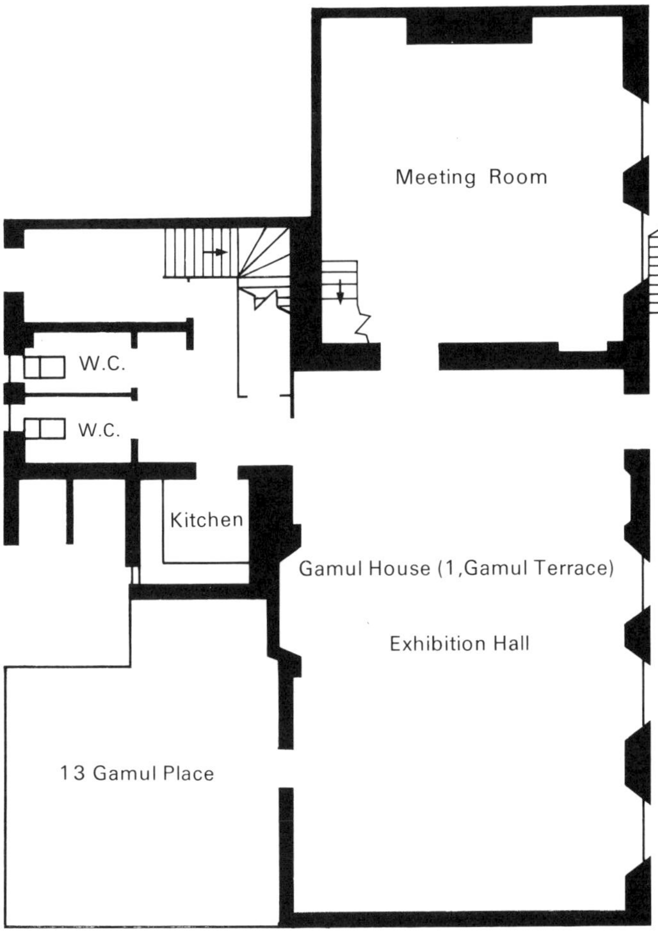

Meeting Room

W.C.

W.C.

Kitchen

Gamul House (1, Gamul Terrace)

Exhibition Hall

13 Gamul Place

FIRST FLOOR PLAN

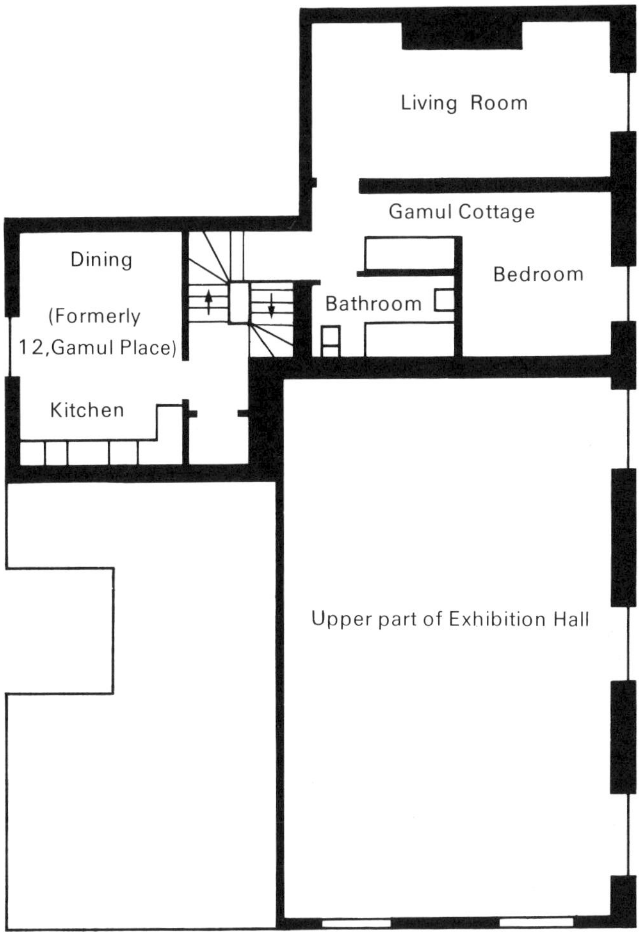

Living Room

Gamul Cottage

Dining
(Formerly
12, Gamul Place)

Bedroom

Bathroom

Kitchen

Upper part of Exhibition Hall

SECOND FLOOR PLAN

GAMUL HOUSE, GAMUL COTTAGE AND
NUMBERS 12 & 13 GAMUL PLACE

Shop
(52)

Shop (54)

Shop (56)

Shop (58)

GROUND FLOOR PLAN
52–58 LOWER BRIDGE STREET

Metres
0   1   2   3   4   5

Yard

Back Room

Original
House

W.C.

Bathroom

TYPICAL GROUND FLOOR PLAN SHOWING
NEW INSIDE LAVATORY, BATH AND KITCHEN
ARRANGEMENT FOR GAMUL TERRACE

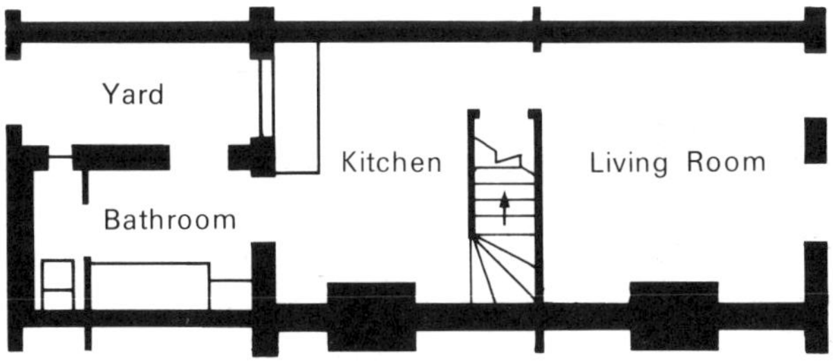

Yard

Kitchen

Living Room

Bathroom

TYPICAL GROUND FLOOR PLAN SHOWING
BATHROOM EXTENSION FOR GAMUL PLACE

Plate 74a The medieval glazing found in the main hall

Plate 74b The restored fireplace

so that the City would not have to pay both a matching grant and a 50 per cent owner's contribution.

Work started in October 1973 and took just over a year. The roof, when opened up, proved to be so badly decayed as to be beyond sensible repair. It was renewed to the same erratic form as the original. The upper section of the street facade had to be rebuilt, and the opportunity was taken to reinstate one of the unusual elliptical windows lighting the top floor. A concealed reinforced concrete ring beam at eaves level and binders at lower levels were necessary to strengthen the weak brick walls. The craftsmen responded well with hand-finished plaster, sensitive handling of the old brickwork and new timberwork with every bit as much quality as the original. A magnificent Jacobean fireplace of carved stone has been cleaned of centuries of paint by a member of the City's Conservation Section. Decorative oak scrolls and ceiling pendants and a bracketed cornice have also been stripped of paint, the oak being simply waxed.

The work revealed both treasures and problems. Two first-floor windows look into the hall; and in one of these old leaded glass was found, suggesting this may have formerly been an open court, only later roofed over to form the hall. The oldest part of the walls is of timber framing, with original wattle-and-daub infilling. A beam in the end

wall suggests the position of an internal Row. On the back of the eighteenth century front door, in its panelled classical surround, a fifteenth century studded oak door was found. Not least among the discoveries were some delightful decorated medieval floor tiles, used to pack up the wallplate when the hall roof was built. All finds have been recorded, and left exposed where possible, this 'archaeological' evidence of the building's varied history being perhaps as important as its present form.

By the end of 1974 it had become obvious that, because of hidden problems and the need to repair Nos. 12 and 13 Gamul Place, which back on to Gamul House, the original estimate would be inadequate. The architect therefore submitted an additional application for aid, as follows:

1: Reinstatement and repair of floor to Gamul House.
2: Repairs to roof and external walls of Nos. 12 and 13 Gamul Place and improvements to No. 13.
3: Conversion of Gamul Cottage to provide a meeting room at first floor level and a flat on the second floor with a new fire-resisting floor between the two.
4: Conversion of No. 12 Gamul Place to provide lavatory accommodation for Gamul House and, on the upper floor, an extension to the flat mentioned above. (This flat is now No. 12 Gamul Place.)
5: Services.

74

6: Conversion of Gamul House into a crafts centre.

These items added £36,450 [£63,788] to the cost, of which £26,750 [£46,813] was eligible for a 50 per cent DOE grant.

Most of the work was completed by June 1975 and during European Architectural Heritage Year the house was in frequent public use for exhibitions and meetings. The Jacobean hall has now been converted into a restaurant.

5.9.2 *Nos. 2–6 Gamul Terrace*

Immediately next to Gamul House, and approached by the same flight of steps, is the late nineteenth century Gamul Terrace. The five houses were built for the married officers stationed at the nearby Castle barracks, while the lower ranks and their wives were accommodated in Gamul Place. Both Nos. 2–6 Gamul Terrace and Nos. 1–11 Gamul Place were dealt with under a single contract and the sixteen houses were included in a General Improvement Area (see 5.9.3 and 5.9.4).

When completed in 1975, the Terrace provided five two-bedroom maisonettes with new bathroom extensions. The work included repointing, repairs to the slates, gutters and chimneys, new timber floors, services and fittings, fire-proofing between the terrace and the shops beneath, and cleaning the elevation to Lower Bridge Street. The original lower floor construction had consisted of large tiles supported on battens fixed to the sides of the joists. The tiles have been relaid in Gamul House.

5.9.3 *Nos. 54–68 Lower Bridge Street and Gamul Cottage (ground floor)*

There is obviously little point in improving the upper floors of a property without looking after the lowest storey, and the City, as owners, were concerned that work should start on Nos. 54–68 Lower Bridge Street, the eight cellar-like shops below. This involved the up-grading and renovation of all these units and the provision of services and toilet facilities in 1979 at a total cost of £53,700, of which £31,456 was eligible for grant aid. Section 10 and Conservation Fund aid has been agreed to cover 50 per cent of the estimated eligible cost. Conversion of the ground floor of the former Gamul Cottage will provide a ninth shop (52 Lower Bridge Street).

These shops form the final element and, when they are complete, the whole Gamul complex will be the largest area of restored property in the Action Area.

5.9.4 *Nos. 1–11 Gamul Place*

Gamul Place forms a secluded court of two-person cottages reached through a 'tunnel' under Gamul Terrace. Whilst none of the houses are of particular historic or architectural value they provide excellent housing accommodation, many of the tenants having lived there all their lives. Gamul Place is also literally irreplaceable because the restrictions of its site and access simply would not allow renewal with modern housing.

The cottages are of solid red brick with Welsh slate roofs, most having a simple plan of two rooms on each floor. Each house originally had only an outside WC and a cold water tap above a stoneware sink in the kitchen. As they also lacked heating and hot water and several were extremely damp and unhealthy, they had earlier been considered for clearance. Despite this threat, the tenants had continued to look after their properties as best they could.

Plate 75a Nos. 2–6 Gamul Terrace, with Nos. 54–68 Lower Bridge Street below

But the consultant's surveys showed that, whilst requiring minor waivers on building regulation standards, the houses could well be improved with grant aid to provide most attractive dwellings. Socially it seemed of prime importance that this existing closely-knit community, largely of elderly people, should not be dispersed.

When work started in February 1974, the tenants realised that the disturbance would be greater than anticipated and agreed – not without some misgivings – to move into alternative accommodation provided by the Housing Department until the work was completed. Their reluctance to move was based on the natural fear that once dispossessed they would be prevented from returning, but each tenant was promised that he or she could return to the same house, and this promise was kept. Work lasted until April 1975 but by careful phasing the tenants were each away for only eight months.

Because many of the tenants had previously carried out their own minor improvements, every effort was made to provide for individuality. Existing shutters and window boxes were kept, and tenants were given the choice of having central heating or retaining their coal fires. They also chose the wallpapers and the colours for their front doors.

Plates 76a to 76d The backyards and kitchens of Gamul Place before and after improvement

Plates 76e and 76f Gamul Place Courtyard before and after landscaping and the construction of the St Mary's housing

Three of the sixteen tenants asked for their houses to be excluded from the original contract. Since then, one tenant has changed her mind, one has died at the age of 97, and one has moved to live with a relative. It was therefore possible to complete these three cottages in 1978.

The work received housing improvement subsidies and the City's share came from the Housing Department's Revenue Account. An interesting but somewhat expensive discovery made during the work was the way in which two walls of No. 1 Gamul Place had been built on infilled medieval cellars; the plan of the cellar bore no relation to the plan of the cottages and extensive underpinning was necessary.

5.9.5 *Gamul Place Courtyard*

The landscaping of the space between the cottages formed a small but significant part of the scheme. The repaving, improved lighting and new planting has greatly enhanced the courtyard and was helped by a Section 10 grant from the DOE. Stones from the Victorian font of St Michael's were re-used to make a bird-bath. Designation of the Gamul Place complex as a General Improvement Area attracted an extra subsidy of £100 per house, and this was used to re-form the back access passages – for many years choked with undergrowth and rubbish.

5.9.6 *Gamul Place Garden*

When the City bought Gamul Place, it had unexpectedly acquired a piece of overgrown land tucked away behind Gamul Place and at that time completely inaccessible. It was decided to open up this area and to make it into a garden both for the children of St Mary's Infant School and for the residents of Gamul Place. Finances were limited, but ways and means of carrying out the work soon appeared.

First on the site were a group of sixth-formers from a local school. Work began in February 1975 when the boys, with axes and shovels, transformed what had previously been an almost impenetrable mass of rubbish and undergrowth into a pleasant open area with the occasional tree; still a long way from being a garden, but a vast improvement on its previous state.

Fortuitously, work had recently started on the southern link of Chester's Outer Ring Road and a large quantity of topsoil thus became readily available. A word with the Contractors and the supply of a lorry to collect the soil plus a 'JCB' earthmover produced a dramatic transformation as the remaining debris disappeared under tons of good Cheshire earth.

Money allocated from City and County funds provided just enough to pay for steps into the garden from the upper level between Castle Street and St Mary's Hill, and also for railings, turf, trees and a path of stepping stones.

Thereafter voluntary help took over again. Once the area of the garden was agreed, the parents and staff of St. Mary's School started fund-raising to buy playground equipment. Their efforts were most successful and, with advice from one of the local authority's conservation assistants they purchased several tons of sandstone blocks, which a valiant group of fathers toiled through several hot Saturdays to turn into a small 'amphitheatre'. A log hut was also bought and assembled by father-power, and the railings were painted by two boys doing Community Service Work. The landscaping was finally completed in January 1977.

Plates 77a and 77b The front and back of Gamul Place after improvement

Plates 77c and 77d Gamul Place Garden during and after landscaping

5.10 The Falcon (Nos. 6–10 Lower Bridge Street)

Attracting grants by setting up an independent Trust

The Falcon is situated at the corner of Lower Bridge Street and Grosvenor Street and is therefore in a key location as one approaches the Action Area from the city centre. It is a handsome, double gabled black-and-white timber structure characteristic of Chester and is probably the most important building in this part of the City. It was originally listed Grade II but was upgraded to I in 1975.

The Falcon is also a key building in this report because of the particular hurdles which had to be overcome before its restoration and future use were assured and because of the complex negotiations involved. The progress of these negotiations has been set down in detail because of their broader application to similar cases elsewhere.

The building consists of four distinct elements:

1. the cellar which, together with the beams of the ground floor, is thirteenth century,
2. the fifteenth to seventeenth century timber-framed house fronting Lower Bridge Street,
3. the sixteenth century timber-framed structure behind, fronting Grosvenor Street.
4. a Victorian shop extension alongside-Nos. 8–10.

Of these, the first two are the most important architecturally. The cellar, with its octagonal stone columns, timber posts and curved braces, is of particular interest. Above it, the fifteenth to seventeenth century structure includes a Row enclosed in 1643 when the property was the town house of the Grosvenor family, and in whose ownership it remained from 1602 until 1979.

In July 1973, the consultants were asked by the owners to consider whether the building, which had been a drapers' store, might be suitable for conversion to a tea room. A scheme was prepared which involved converting

Plate 78a The Falcon before the sashes were removed in 1893

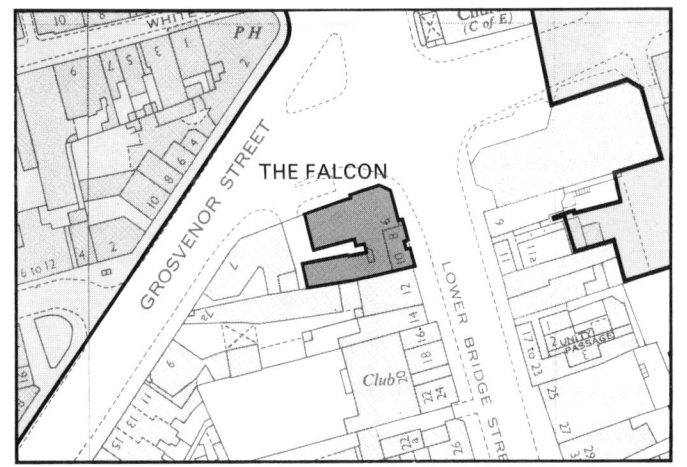

Plate 79a The same view a few years ago

the old cellar into a coffee bar directly accessible from the street, opening up the original Row, and providing steps at ground level and offices above, with stores and toilets at the rear.

However, a preliminary survey brought to light several serious defects, and the consultants obtained permission to undertake a far more detailed investigation, including opening up a great deal of the structure.

The defects were found to be the compounded results of centuries of inadequate maintenance and haphazard rebuilding and repair. Excessive alterations and reconstruction bore little or no relation to the earlier parts of the structure below, a main structural post was found to rest only on floorboards, and a stone pier was resting on a small timber lintel. A doubling-up of roof timbers over the original members had increased the loading, which was

already transferred eccentrically down through the jettied front – and the result had been a failure of the main ground floor beam. Vibrations set up by heavy traffic on the widened Grosvenor Street had added to the problems, while the gabled roof brought the usual corollary of leaking valley gutters, with resultant wet rot and beetle infestation.

In July 1974, the consultants produced an estimate of their proposals as follows:

Element	Repair	Conversion	Total
Lower Bridge St. frontage	35,000	13,000	48,000
Grosvenor Street frontage	28,000	17,800	45,800
Cellar	37,000	5,800	42,800
Total cost: No. 6 Lower Bridge St.	100,000	36,600	136,600
1979 Equivalent	*175,000*	*64,000*	*239,000*

The above figures exclude fees and VAT.

The scheme prepared at this stage also included additional costs associated with works to the Victorian shops adjoining and a rear extension. These works, increased the cost to about £200,000 [350,000] exclusive of fees and VAT.

This estimate was considerably in excess of the probable capital value of the property after conversion, so, as a means of bridging the gap and increasing the viability of the scheme the consultants proposed, firstly, that the fullest use be made of all available grants and loans and, secondly, that the work be phased over five years in such a way that some sections could be made available for letting before the completion of the entire contract.

Plate 79b Location map

A contribution was sought from the Department of the Environment, but the latter were placed in a dilemma because of their policy of not awarding grants to individuals or organisations which, like the Grosvenor Estate, possessed the financial resources to undertake the work at their own expense. This restriction looked like endangering the entire project until the consultants suggested that the property be handed over to a non-profit making trust formed specifically to undertake the work. The Grosvenor Estate, however, were at first reluctant to hand over property and funds to an organisation which in the long-term might not be financially viable.

The consultants pointed out that, if the whole project was not to be undermined, emergency repairs would have to be carried out immediately. In November 1976, the DOE agreed to provide a 100 per cent grant of £5,000 [£8,300] for this work. In 1977 the Grosvenor Estate re-applied for a grant towards the cost of repairs. The proposals were limited to No. 6 Lower Bridge Street. A revised estimate of the cost of repairs submitted in 1978 came to £161,000 [£209,000]. Progress was being made with setting up the Trust and the DOE therefore offered a Section 4 grant representing half the repair cost.

Meanwhile the Estate was pursuing negotiations with Samuel Smith Old Brewery (Tadcaster) who were prepared to make a substantial capital contribution to the cost of the restoration and conversion in return for a long lease at a nominal rent.

These negotiations were completed in August 1978. It was another year, however, before the Falcon Trust was firmly established and the end of 1979 before tenders could be received. The lowest of these was £193,000 plus fees and VAT, making a total of £262,470. To offset this, the following pattern of financial support had been agreed:

	£
Contributions by the Grosvenor Estate	42,500
Purchase of lease by brewery	55,000
DOE Section 4 grant	85,000
Chester City Conservation Fund	34,500
Contribution by the Pilgrim Trust	3,000
Total	£220,000

In the hope that the shortfall of £42,470 would be met with the help of additional grant aid, the Trust accepted the tender on 14 January 1980 and work commenced to bring the building back into active use. The final scheme prepared by the consultants comprises a public house at ground floor level with cellarage below and a three-bedroom flat and meeting room above. It is scheduled for completion early in 1982.

Plate 80a Plans and main facade of The Falcon

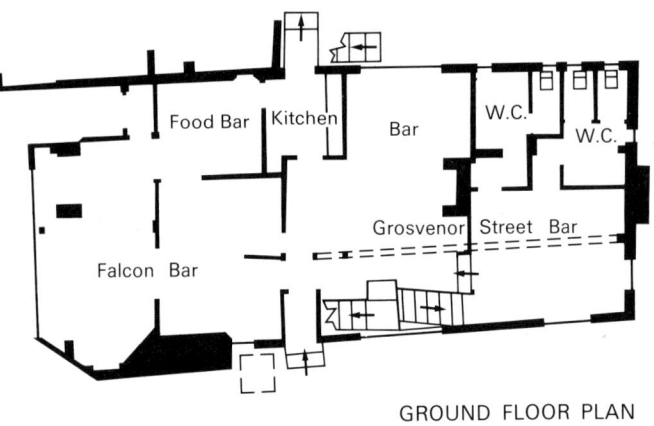

GROUND FLOOR PLAN

FIRST FLOOR PLAN

CELLAR PLAN

Plate 81a The Grosvenor Street frontage

Plate 81b The top of Lower Bridge Street

Plate 82a Nos. 90–92 Lower Bridge Street before restoration

6 An owner's view of the conservation process

The following account of the purchase, restoration and conversion of Nos. 90–92 Lower Bridge Street is largely based on extracts from the correspondence and notes of Mr and Mrs Eaton, the present owners, and reveals the problems and successes of such an enterprise from the point of view of the user and occupier, instead of that of the professional or government officer.

6.1 The initial decision

Between the Bear and Billet and Ye Olde Edgar, both fine half-timbered buildings, are two somewhat plainer houses, Nos. 90 and 92 Lower Bridge Street. Their typical early nineteenth century brick facades hide good plaster-work and panelling which survived a dubious conversion into two 'front room' shops with living accommodation behind and above. By the time of the 1968 Report, the premises were empty and semi-derelict and the consultants put forward proposals for their further conversion and restoration. The scheme indicated how it and other similar properties could be brought back to life, but the idea was not taken up. In 1970 the licensee of the Bear and Billet public house considered using the building as an hotel extension, and in the 1971 Interim Report the consultants supported the proposal. As finances were available, they recommended that the City purchase both properties and investigate a lease-back arrangement.

However, the 1973 Report was obliged to acknowledge that the houses were still threatened by defects and their condition had continued to deteriorate. That year, therefore, the City purchased Nos. 90 and 92 for £26,300 [£53,390] in a block purchase which included Ye Olde Edgar and Nos. 3–5 Shipgate Street. They intended to repair and re-sell them: but in the 1976 Report the consultants noted that all negotiations with interested parties had fallen through. As the repair work was not implemented, straight away the buildings continued to deteriorate; severe defects including dry rot were accelerating and tending to spread to other properties, thereby reducing the possibilities of re-sale.

At the beginning of 1977 Mr and Mrs Eaton approached the conservation officer in the hope of finding a building suitable for conversion into a pottery, shop and family house. Nos. 90–92 was one of two properties he suggested.

Despite having serious doubts about the condition of the property and after giving it a great deal of careful thought, they wrote to the Council as follows:

> Margaret and Tony Eaton, of Coed yr Allt, Gwernymynydd, would like to buy the above property, and, after extensive renovation and repair have been carried out, to use the ground floor for a studio pottery and show room, (possibly with workshop accommodation for other craftsmen in wood, metal, stone, or fabric etc) with living accommodation for their family – five children aged between 8–18 years – on the first and second floors, as shown on the outline proposal plans attached.
>
> These ideas have been discussed with the Conservation Officer, after an initial inspection of the property; the present condition of the building is such that much of it will have to

be reconstructed, keeping the facade, basic structure, and interesting features such as beams etc, intact; however, as the prospective buyers also have a deep interest in conservation, agreement on these points should not prove difficult.

> It is the intention that the studio pottery will be a family affair and will not create a 'factory'; the kilns would be fired by electricity, and no processes likely to be detrimental to the environment would be used.
>
> The finances of such a project are likely to prove difficult, of course, but Tony Eaton already has £1,000 worth of pottery equipment, and it is understood that under the Bridgegate Action Area Conservation Scheme, such a rescue project as that now proposed for Ye Old Edgar would, if approved, qualify for grants allocated on the basis of the owners financing 50 per cent of the work, and the Department of the Environment and the City Council contributing 25 per cent each. Mr and Mrs Eaton would therefore make a nominal offer of £500 for the freehold of the derelict property, which would leave £7,000 in cash to get the work underway immediately, to be augmented by a further £5,000 to £6,000 cash on the sale of the Eaton family's present dwelling.... but an assurance of sympathetic consideration of an application to the Council for a mortgage to complete the work would be a necessary ingredient of the scheme.
>
> If any further information is required, would you please communicate with the Eatons immediately so that the points of this proposition may be considered, and hopefully, agreed to in principle, in order that the second stage – that of engaging the services of a quantity surveyor to draw up plans and estimates for the proposed conversion and restoration – may proceed as quickly as possible, before the roof caves in!

The conservation officer had advised them on the problems and potential of the site and of the correct procedures to be taken to obtain the maximum likely grant aid and on 18 January Mrs Eaton wrote:

> It is of vital importance to us that we would have these proposals accepted in principle, especially the freehold price, Department of the Environment and City Council grants, and the assurance of a mortgage, before we proceed to the next vital stage of a detailed quantity survey with itemised estimation of costs.

The Eatons contacted their architect who inspected the building. Despite the failure to arrange a Council mortgage they decided to carry on. On 2 February, Mrs Eaton wrote stating that the architect had started on the plans and asked to see the deeds:

> ... as it appears that there are useful outbuildings which could store materials, house the kilns etc, and presumably the extent of these would be shown on the deeds?
>
> There is the question of clearance of rubbish to be considered, which would make the costing job of the architect and building contractors so very much easier – we could perhaps do the actual clearing if the Council would provide skips for the removal of rubbish?

The complications of taking on such an ambitious project are well illustrated by this further letter of 16 February:

> Thank you for the useful meeting last week; it is good to know that the D of E is thinking of giving a 50 per cent grant

Plate 84a (*above*) The bottom of Lower Bridge Street in 1860: No. 90–92 is on the right.

Plate 84b (*left*) The facade after restoration.

Plate 84c The first floor living room.

towards the scheme – but could you please specify: 50 per cent *of what* exactly? It is also helpful to know that the Council may be able to find some grant aid possible, especially if, as you suggested, trying to obtain improvement grants towards the heating, drainage, and electrical installations so vital to the rehabilitation scheme for the above building, is likely to take such a long time that it would ruin our proposed time scale for the scheme.

We have now settled a price, and come to a 'gentleman's agreement' with the people who are keen to buy our house here in Gwernynydd, but they would dearly like to be in by Christmas of this year – and of course, that would also be good for us, and our hoped for trade, to open for the festive season.

We are also exploring the possibilities of loans, to 'top up' our total capital to £18,500 – the Building Societies are not helpful; Tony has found that his superannuation is frozen; but the Craft Advisory Committee will give some loans – interest payable, but repaid as a grant at the end of the five year period; our solicitor is very helpful – and we could always float ourselves as a small company – how many shares would you like?

We really are totally committed to this whole scheme, and do hope that between ourselves, Chester City Council, and the Department of the Environment, we shall be able to renovate, rejuvenate, and make use of this very interesting building.

The Eatons were to discover that they were unable to obtain a house improvement grant because the combined rateable values of Nos. 90 and 92 exceeded the maximum laid down for house improvement grant availability.

6.2 Problems

The first major stumbling block occurred in March when the Eatons received an estimate for the conversion of £60,000 [£89,000], fifty per cent more than they had budgeted for. They therefore went back to their architect and asked him to prepare a revised, less ambitious scheme, and to obtain comprehensive estimates. On 25 March, Mrs Eaton wrote:

I have an appointment to see our Solicitor to put him more fully into the picture on Monday; I also have ready a set of revised plans plus the completed official application form for the £5,000 mortgage which the Cheshire Building Society have agreed to 'consider favourably', and I shall hand these into the Mold Office when we know the outcome of the planning consent request. The Manager explained that although the mortgage can only be granted on the completed property, when we have official offer of the mortgage, this will stand as surety for a bridging loan, so to speak, between paying for the work to be done, and completion.

I shall look forward to meeting you next Thursday, then, to sort out, as far as we can, 1. the scale of priorities of work to be done; 2. the areas of joint financial responsibility; 3. the phasing of work and payment; and 4. the steps in the legal formalities to be undertaken to get the scheme underway. Again, many thanks for all your hard work towards shaping reality from our dream!

The first estimates for the revised schemes came to £49,000 [£73,000], exclusive of such items as a new damp course and woodwork treatment. In a letter to their architect, Mrs Eaton explained that the contractor

.... feels that the idea of taking out all the existing doors and windows on the back wall, blocking-up and re-opening for new window and door positions, is 'slightly mad'; he suggests, subject to the opinion of the structural engineer of course, that the structure should be disturbed as little as possible, and that to repoint, put in new window and door frames into existing spaces, and even to use extra tie bars if considered necessary, would be much better both for the general health of the

building, and the prospects of being able to do it at all!

We are now feeling a little depressed, because it now looks as though this 'ideal position' for our scheme may be far beyond our reach – as you know, at the moment, our prospects of money available for everything stands at about £18,500 – including freehold, costs, fees, removal etc etc and even if we could somehow raise another £1,500 – £2,000 to bring us up to our original £20,000 'guestimate', if all this resulted in a sound, but unfinished, shop and accommodation, which needed not only a lot of work, but a lot of cash for materials, to complete, plus heavy rates and mortgage and loan repayments, – we could have ploughed all our assets into a mill-stone....

At the beginning of April, things took a few steps forward when the Development and Planning Committee gave planning permission for the architect's latest scheme, agreed to let Eatons have the house for only £500, and to provide them with a City Conservation Fund grant of £5,000. Back in July 1975 the Council had recommended selling Nos. 90–92 for £5,250 and, in persuading the City to part with it for less than one tenth of that figure, the conservation officer had emphasised the rapidity of the deterioration and the increasing threat to the adjoining buildings. The architect was therefore asked to produce yet another scheme, this time based on a total cost of £40,000 [£59,000]. The plans and specifications were progressing satisfactorily when, on 17 May, the Building Society refused to make a loan, so the Eatons tried the bank.

20 May 77:
Saw Midland Bank Manager... willing to give us an overdraft as 'trading facility' (?). He would want deeds 90–92 as collateral, second mortgage on Coe yr Allt (our Welsh home) for bridging loan, photostats of grant aid offers, and estimates.

23 June 77:
I have been through the costing specification and, by chopping off all the painting, wood preserving, clearance and minor demolition (cupboards, tiles from floors etc) in the interior, which we can tackle ourselves, I have saved quite a bit.

... as soon as we have something settled, we mean to go in there and get started on the cleaning.

6.3 Starting work

At the end of June the Eatons obtained permission from the City to start clearing out the rubbish, and at the end of July they decided to call in the contractors to make the roof weathertight. The City, as owners, were agreeable provided the Eatons 'indemnify the Council against any loss or damages occasioned by the carrying out of the works'. This elicited an immediate response from Mrs Eaton:

We thank you for your letter of agreement and approval for work to be started on the roof of the above property; however, we would like to point out that the works already undertaken, and those envisaged, far from causing 'any loss or damage' can only result in additional value and improvement, and we would like to put on record the following facts about the condition of the building when we started clearance work in July: over the past years during which the property has been standing empty and neglected,
1. Vandals have removed pipes, wiring, lead fireplaces, etc.
2. Squatters have removed, and burned, floor and skirting boards, panelling, cupboards, doors and banisters.
3. Most of the glass, and some of the window frames have gone from the back of the house.
4. The suspended ceilings on the top floor have recently fallen in, revealing missing tiles (slates), allowing rain to penetrate, and much of the plasterwork is cracked, loose, and falling.
5. The remains of the roof drainage system is now channelling

Plate 86a Restored interior, now the Three Kings Studios

Plate 86b Location map

Plate 86c Bateman's drawing of Nos. 86–96 Lower Bridge
Street

Plate 86d Plans of Nos. 90–92 Lower Bridge Street after
conversion

GROUND FLOOR PLAN

FIRST FLOOR PLAN

SECOND FLOOR PLAN

Metres
0 1 2 3 4 5 6 7 8 9 10

the rain that is collected into the structure of the building.

6. The vegetation allowed to proliferate in the back yard (including the now mature sycamore trees, and three foot depth of debris) has damaged the primitive drainage system, and added to the dampness of the rear walls.

7. The false chipboard on 2×2 floor put down by the Council over an original board floor already badly affected by wet rot, encouraged a bad infestation of dry rot, which has developed rapidly in the shop and hallway of No. 92.

We have noticed a marked deterioration of the property since we first became interested in January of this year, and feel that far from any 'loss or damaged occasioned by the carrying out of the works' occurring, we have already done much to add to the value and halt the damage by removing six builder's skip loads of rubbish; vegetation; worm eaten furniture; wet feather and straw mattresses; the timber floors affected by the wet and dry rot; piles of bricks heaped on the floor from the removal of the old fireplaces; soggy plaster lying on the board floors upstairs etc etc ...

The only likely reason of our withdrawal from the scheme to renovate and refurbish 90/92 Lower Bridge Street would be the insufficient, or refusal of, grants from the Department of the Environment or the Council of the City of Chester ...... and as undoubtedly, the Council would have to do something this winter to make the roof weatherproof to avoid further deterioration and damage to adjoining properties, the work we are doing at the moment is merely progressing towards this end.

We do appreciate the efforts of the Council, as present owners, and therefore interested party, to help us to get this scheme underway, and we hope to hear good news about the finalising of the necessary grants in the very near future.

The contractors started work on 12 September, by which time the Eatons had cleared out most of the refuse and were acting virtually as unpaid sub-contractors: removing infested timber, demolishing unwanted partitions, etc. The contractors planned to complete the work in April 1978.

On 14 September the DOE replied to the City's request for a Town Scheme grant with an offer of £5,000 [£7,400], ie , 25 per cent of the cost of repairs estimated at £21,531 [£32,080]. With a matching City contribution this would meet 50 per cent, but would not cover the cost of conversion or improvement. Grant aid for the latter is not normally available from Town Scheme or Section 10 conservation sources, so the City wrote to the DOE for help towards the cost of conversion (£22,550 [£33,600]) and fittings (£2,520 [£3,755]).

6.4 A 'slight disaster'

On the night of Friday 27 October there occurred what the architect described as a 'slight disaster'. As a result of high winds the chimney to the rear of No. 90 collapsed, crashing into the building, badly damaging the roof, partly destroying the second floor and completely destroying the first floor.

He noted in his site minutes of 1 November:

The assembled company viewed this collapse pensively. It had been noted prior to the collapse that the flue at second floor level was not 'tied' to the outside wall but it was staggering to see that it had collapsed so completely. It was a sobering thought however that the collapse happened when no-one was on site.

The immediate problem was to support the roof and stabilise the rear wall. A system of raking shores outside and beams inside was agreed upon. The re-creation of a sound building also entailed the re-building of the rear walls and substantial areas of flooring.

The Eatons had not insured against storm damage and the additional cost was estimated at about £6,250 [£9,312]. They re-examined their financial position and wrote to the Council as follows on 6 November:

We feel that it would be financial suicide to borrow any more money to add to our original stake of £20,000 for the following reasons:

1. Overdraft facilities can be withdrawn at will at short notice;
2. Not only is the interest based on the current bank rate repayable, but repayment of the capital is also required.
3. The Chester Valuation Department has assessed the rateable value of the completed property, based on the plans provided, at £722, and the commercial rate is approximately 103p in the pound at present.
4. The comprehensive insurance cover, bearing in mind the timber construction, and escalating rebuilding costs, will obviously carry a substantial yearly premium, and
5. For the project to be commercially viable, we must be able to cover our costs as we built up custom and goodwill in a hitherto derelict site position.

However, as you well know, we have already spent a great deal of time, effort, and now, money, on this project since its initiation last January: we are captivated by the house, and we have built all our hopes and dreams for the future into the success of its renovation.

One unfortunate aspect of this setback is that we had already cut out all ideas not absolutely vital to the restoration of the structure and its future use; also, although we have, as a family, already done much of the clearance and preparation for the contractor's skilled workmen, and plan to do the bulk of the internal decorating ourselves, these savings have already been taken into account.

Thus the only areas we can now look to for a saving are the more personal near essential non-eligible ones:

1. We can forego kitchen units, floor coverings, tiling to bathrooms and sinks, even door handles, and curtain tracking;
2. It may be possible to make a small saving by incorporating the rear first floor stairway with the building of the new buttresses;
3. Several friends have offered to help us to move our belongings, when the time comes, without incurring the expense of a removals firm .....

but all these items together will only free, at most, £750. We have, therefore, once more to look to the generosity of Chester City Council, and would ask you, as conservation officer, to explain the grave difficulties now facing the project, which have arisen from this totally unexpected calamity.

The following day the City wrote to the DOE requesting assistance towards the repair of the chimney, but to ensure the safety of the rear of the building the contractor was obliged to start the repairs before the promise of additional grant aid. Mrs Eaton therefore wrote to the Council:

If, contrary to your assured expectations, Chester City Council and the DOE *cannot* regard our request sympathetically, and thus we are forced to withdraw from the project for lack of necessary funds, then the roof and structure would, in any case, have required the present works undertaken to render them sound, and would be the responsibility of the Council, as owners.

This letter highlights the fact that, although the Eatons were employing a contractor to renovate Nos. 90 and 92 and were carrying out a great deal of the work themselves, the properties were still in the Council's ownership and, if the Eatons had to withdraw, the authority would have to foot the entire bill and not just the proportion so far offered in grant aid.

However, a Section 10 grant of £15,000 [£22,350] towards the work had meanwhile been agreed by the

Historic Buildings Council and confirmation was sent on 15 November. A few days later, the DOE was also able to confirm an additional Town Scheme grant towards the repair of the chimney.

6.5 Success at last

With the assurance of adequate aid, the Eatons were able to complete the purchase of the property on 17 February 1978 (and arrange insurance cover against fire, storm, vandalism etc). The family moved in one month later and the contractor completed his work on the first and second floors in May. The shop finally opened to the public in July 1978. Despite the additional cost of the chimney repair, cost-cutting elsewhere reduced the overall cost by £3,000, the final figure being £49,600.

In September and October 1978 the Heritage Centre held an exhibition of photographs and plans of Nos. 90–92 before, during and after the repair and conversion, together with various items unearthed during the work. In December 1979 the Eatons received a Conservation Award from Chester City Council. In March 1980, during the course of the Secretary of State's visit to Chester, he took the opportunity of seeing the property and meeting the Eatons. Mr and Mrs Eaton subsequently wrote to him about their experience and what they felt could be learned from it: They made a number of suggestions:

The public should be kept informed of the opportunities available, that is, of
1. Listed Buildings in public (and private?) ownership in need of conservation, renovation, and new purpose;
2. the possible levels of grant aid available;
3. the possibilities of saving on the initial estimate by family involvement in planning, clearance and labouring, careful removal of items to be restored, supervision and co-ordination, and final restoration and decoration after the contractors have completed the main works; in this context,

it would be useful to compile a list of architects and contractors prepared to work in this way, and to keep records of past projects for reference; finally,
4. the availability of Council mortgages, or the ready provision of documents on grant aid etc, to convince Bank managers that such a scheme is well worthy of a loan.

In his reply, the Secretary of State expressed his sympathy with their suggestions:

It was most encouraging to see such a splendid example of conservation in action. I am very pleased that the Department were able to help, but without the vision, practical skills and hard work of the Eaton family and the determination to succeed that overcame all the problems which faced you, the building would not have been so painstakingly restored.
I agree with you that it is important to capture the imagination of the public and arouse their enthusiasm for the task.

He then referred to the work of the Historic Buildings Bureau in publicising Listed Buildings available for sale and made mention of publications which list the various forms of grant aid for historic buildings, in particular, the leaflet brochure produced by the Civic Trust.

The difficulty about giving wider publicity to the availability of grants at the present time is that for several years the number of applications has outstripped the funds available and with limited staff resources as well, it would be unfortunate if we stimulated interest only to have to say later that we could not help. For this reason we tend to concentrate the major part of the resources available for grants in towns such as Chester where the local authority are invited to prepare a programme of work each year. Even if we were able to increase the funds available – and it is difficult enough to keep them at their present level – we could not hope to do all the work necessary by financial assistance from Government sources alone. This is why it is so important to harness all the energies and talents of people like you who can do so much themselves and put the available funds to such good use.

7 Experience in Chester: ten lessons

What can be learned from ten years experience of an active Conservation Programme in Chester? These are some of the main lessons, and they are applicable in any historic town.

7.1 Relate to region

A conservation programme designed to tackle the problems of any declining historic area must form part of an overall planning policy. We should first understand the whole town, the way its parts are related to each other and its role in regional and national terms. Then we can begin to understand the special pressures upon it and to identify its strengths and weaknesses. If anything is to be achieved 'on the ground', this broader study must be a first step and not an end in itself.

In Chester, this was done by the 1968 Conservation Study, and the Structure and District Plans have since amplified and updated the context for conservation.

7.2 Allocate funds

A specific allocation of funds is needed to get things moving. But this can do much to attract private money, so that a significant impact can be made without causing local authorities to exceed their spending targets.

Chester's decision to levy a Conservation Rate has been fundamental to success. Many local authorities could usefully follow this pioneering move. By providing a fund 'at home', the City has attracted aid from central government, and has prompted valuable private investment. The budget has been regularly increased to keep pace with inflation, and any unspent balance of the annual allocation is carried over into the next year.

7.3 Organise a conservation team

Results can only be achieved when specific people are allocated for the job. An 'inside' man, such as a Conservation Officer, can provide a link between the Town Hall and the people concerned. There are advantages in having an 'outside' view as well. A consultant architect can lend stature to the Conservation viewpoint and help create a spirit of trust, when the programme is in its most critical stages. This arrangement also provides flexibility and may reduce the need to take on new and permanent staff.

In Chester, the combination of a Conservation Section within the Local Authority and independent consultants has succeeded in promoting a vigorous programme of action.

7.4 Hold regular action area meetings

Setting up a working party of those concerned will enable everyone to maintain contact. Regular meetings resulting in a clear allocation of tasks will then keep things moving.

In Chester, the working party includes legal, valuation and conservation expertise. Representatives of the City's Housing Department, the County Council and the DOE Headquarters and Regional Offices also attend as the occasion demands.

7.5 Gather facts and knowledge

To revitalise a declining area calls for a special concentration of energy and effort. Facts and informed opinions must be collected not only about the use and condition of every building, but also about the hopes and plans of every owner and occupant. Situations affecting individual properties can change suddenly and dramatically; vigilance is essential if one is to seize opportunities as they occur.

In the 1968 Report, Bridgegate was identified as in danger and in urgent need of a Conservation Action Programme. More detailed information was gathered in preparing the 1971 Report, which provided the basis for crucial decisions.

7.6 Declare public commitment

Uncertainty and fear can cause blight and discourage building care, To counter these, the Local Authority must declare and publicise a clear policy for the area. In this way they can instil a sense of security among residents and users and create the right atmosphere for action.

In Bridgegate this policy was first expressed when the City acquired key properties to combat pressures for demolition and redevelopment. The policy was fully clarified in the 1973 Action Plan.

7.7 Firm strategy – flexible tactics

Within a firm strategy, flexible and responsive tactics will enable each opportunity for positive action to be taken as it arises. Flexibility may be needed in applying housing policy, land use zoning and the criteria for grant aid.

In Bridgegate, housing once deemed to have no future will now be kept and improved, and shielded from the tide of earlier commercial and office encroachment. Adaptability to circumstances undoubtedly saved a number of buildings at critical stages, for example by giving grants and loans to cover the cost of survey, acquisition and emergency repairs.

All these tactics reflect exceptional circumstances which justified a departure from the norm. But the overall policy and strategy have remained rock-like through all the vicissitudes of administrative change and economic recession.

7.8 Set example and help others to follow

Someone has to make the first move; this must almost invariably be the local authority. It is not enough simply to produce a plan and expect private owners to start implementing it immediately. An 'examplar' scheme will help to inspire others by showing just what can be done.

In saving buildings like the Gamul group, Chester has demonstrated wide ranging types of conservation—historic building repair, house improvement, new infill development, selective clearance of eyesores, and landscaping.

7.9 Guide and encourage

To achieve conservation, a local authority can use its emergency powers. Among these are Compulsory Purchase Orders and Repairs Notices. But the goodwill of the neighbourhood is so important that every effort should be made to achieve the desired ends without having to resort to statutory powers. Much more often the need is to guide those who are unsure as to how to proceed and perhaps apprehensive about committing themselves to restoring and letting their premises.

In Chester, it has not yet been necessary to apply these reserve powers: but readiness to use them has on occasion prompted a willingness on the part of the owner to negotiate. As elsewhere, the planning staff are ready to discuss problems and proposals informally, and can provide a leaflet on the financial aid available. But the City goes one step further: it enables its consultants to prepare ideas and sketch schemes at no charge to the owner. In this way, he can be helped to appreciate the latent potential of his property.

7.10 Enlist public support and participation

The love of one's home and town is a deep instinct, and the public expect to have a say in matters affecting the environment. This expectation is reflected in the multitude of civic and amenity societies and residents' groups found throughout the land. Public participation from an early stage, with constant liaison and response, will succeed in mobilizing local feeling.

Chester calls on the services of a Conservation Area Advisory Committee and enjoys good relations with the Chester Civic Trust and the Cheshire Society of Architects. The Heritage Centre has a frequently updated exhibition displaying conservation projects and has provided a centre for discussion on major planning issues. Close links are maintained with the local press and a Newsletter keeps everyone informed of progress.

Chester is unique: but the problems of the Bridgegate Area are typical of those found in historic towns across the country and throughout the world.

Ten years of experience now demonstrates some of the ways in which we can help these neglected areas back to life, and bring out their special qualities. But this can only be achieved when money and effort are harnessed to a concerted programme of conservation action, backed by a real public concern.

Acknowledgements

The authors are grateful to the following organisations and individuals for their generous help in the preparation of this report:

All members of Donald W. Insall and Associates concerned in the continuing Chester Conservation Programme.

Chester City Council, especially their Directorate of Technical Services, for constant assistance and encouragement and for access to their correspondence.

Cheshire County Council for their help in the preparation of the text.

Leonard W. Baart, BArch FRIBA FIArb for his help in the preparation of the text for The Bear and Billet (No. 94 Lower Bridge Street), and for his permission to reproduce the survey drawing of the front elevation.

P. N. Bartlett Esq for his help in the preparation of the text for Nos. 70–74 Lower Bridge Street and Nos. 15–17 and 25 Castle Street.

James Brotherhood DipArch RIBA for his help in the preparation of the text for No. 53 and Nos. 54–68 Lower Bridge Street and Nos. 20 and 22 Castle Street, and for permission to reproduce the survey drawings of No. 53 Lower Bridge Street.

Mrs Margaret Eaton for her help in the preparation of the text for the Three Kings Studios (Nos. 90–92 Lower Bridge Street) and for permission to quote extracts from her correspondence with Chester City Council and her architect, Gordon Punt RIBA.

Larkfield Properties and T. K. Skinner and Associates for the details and drawings of No. 11A Lower Bridge Street.

Northwest Regional Office, DOE, for their assistance in preparing details of costs and grants.

Valerie F. Warren, FSAI, for the drawings on pages 10, 25, 88 and back cover.

Appendix A: Contract record form

Draft form for completion by architect in charge of job, and for future reference on the capacities of contractors employed.

Date . . . .

Part 1

Job . . . .

Value of job . . . .

Type of contract (fixed price or cost-plus etc):

. . . .

Type of building . . . .

Trades concerned:

Mason . . . .   Names . . . .

. . . .

. . . .

. . . .

Foreman . . . .   Trade . . . .

Surveyor or cost clerk . . . .

Special capacities required . . . .

. . . .

to . . . .

Costs: contracted . . . .

Eventual . . . .

Notes . . . .

Part 2 Contract record (confidential)

Adequacy and standard of trades in opinion of architect:	*Percentage assessed eg 50% 100%*
Mason	. . . .
. . . .	. . . .
. . . .	. . . .
. . . .	. . . .

Adequacy and standard of management and control:	
Estimating	. . . .
Site supervision	. . . .
Cost control	. . . .
Delivery/quality of materials	. . . .
Programming and promises	. . . .
Guarantees and maintenance	. . . .
Corespondence	. . . .
Final accounts	. . . .

Notes: Job conditions, adverse and otherwise . . . .

. . . .

. . . .

Referees (subject to the courtesy of forewarning by architects): . . . .

. . . .

Appendix B: Historic building record forms

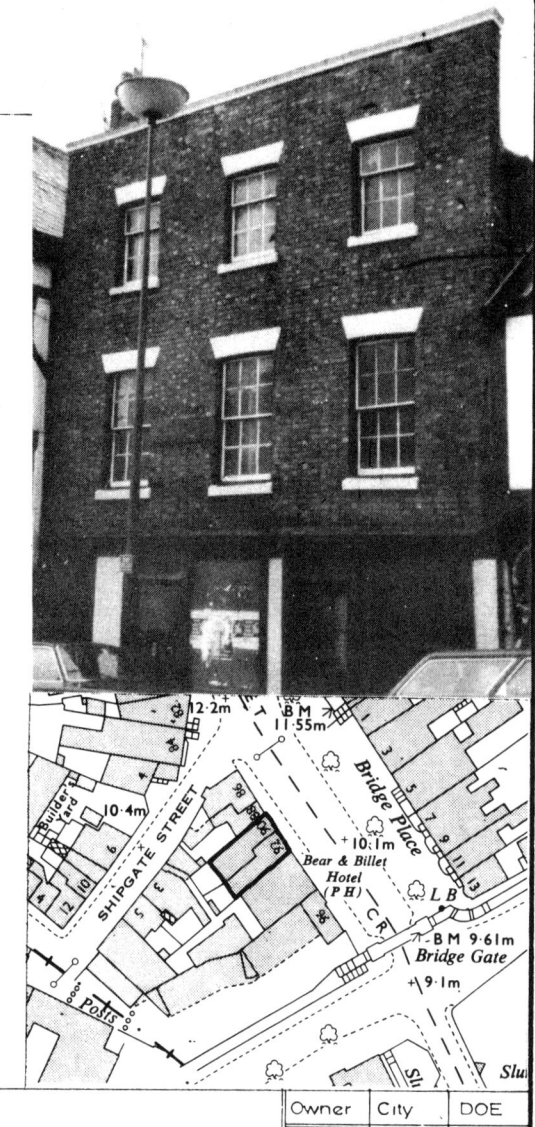

LOCATION

90 & 92 LOWER BRIDGE STREET

ASSESSMENT

Listed Grade II. Early 19th century facade covers two earlier buildings – remnants of original timber framing in side walls.

<u>1967</u> – buildings empty and semi-derelict.

<u>1976</u> – still empty and in state of advanced decay.

Buildings purchased by Council in 1973 from owner reluctant to re-habilitate. Intention was to repair and resell but so far all negotiations with interested parties have fallen through.

Condition continues to deteriorate, severe defects (including dry rot) are accelerating and tending to spread to adjacent properties.

Possibilities for re-sale continue to decrease.

City Council ownership.

RECOMMENDATION	Owner	City	DOE
1 First Aid – investigate and remedy dry rot and water penetration. <u>This work must be done urgently not only for the benefit of this building but to prevent spread of decay to adjoining buildings.</u>		●	
2 Complete repair and rehabilitation scheme can probably only be resolved when future of land at rear has been determined as part of Action Area Study.		●	

ACTION AND FINANCE	Owner	City	DOE
1 First Aid – Council should give early priority to including finance in Capital Estimates.		●	●
2 Complete repair scheme – possibly Section 10 grants to assist with re-planning and user requirements.		●	●

Bibliography and credits

National Pilot Study

Chester: A Study in Conservation. Report to the Minister of Housing and Local Government and the City of Chester by Donald W. Insall & Associates HMSO 1968.

Bridgegate: interim reports

Two reports were printed in very limited edition: they comprise a Survey and Action Plan for Bridgegate respectively. A few copies are still available.

Bridgegate Action Programme: Interim Report 1: December 1971

Bridgegate Action Programme: Interim Report 2: February 1973

Conference and discussion papers

Produced and available (although unpublished):

The Survey of Historic Towns – The Chester Study for the SPAB Conference for Planning & Conservation Officers, on *The Regeneration of Historic Centres,* November 1975. Verbatim notes, unillustrated. *Chester – Stop the Rot,* (under-use of upper floors): April 1980. Available from Donald W. Insall & Associates.

Conservation progress review

The Review of Progress in the Conservation Programme, undertaken in 1976 under joint sponsorship of the DOE and the City, by the consultants together with the Dept. of Technical Services. The reports relate to the City and rural areas respectively.

Chester: Conservation Review Study 1976, Chester City Council.

Rural Areas: Conservation Review Study 1976, Chester City Council.

Reports

Proposals for the Revitalisation of Shipgate Street, Chester. The Director of Technical Services, Chester City Council and Donald W. Insall & Associates. November 1978. Unpublished.

Articles, lectures etc (including reprints)

Action for Conservation: Chester: Britain's Historic Towns: A Pilot Study by Donald Insall. Reprinted from Journal of the Royal Town Planning Institute: July/Aug 1970.

Progress in Chester. Reprinted from Civic Trust Newsletter, March 1972.

Pride Returns to Chester: Progress in Conservation, Thomas Whiting, Country Life, 22 February 1973.

Chester: Conservation in Practice by D. Anne Dennier. Reprint from Town Planning Review, Vol 46 No. 4, October 1975.

Heritage City by David Crawford: Reprint from Building, 5 February 1976.

Five Years of Steady Progress: The Bridgegate, Chester, Michael Wright, Country Life, 4 March 1976.

Chester: The Story of a Research Operation by Tony Aldous. Reprint from Illustrated London News, 1977.

Chester Old and New, David Crawford, The Architect, May 1977.

Chester: Ten Years After, Gillian Darley, The Architects' Journal, 10 May 1978.

Approaches to Progress: York and Chester – I, John Cornforth, Country Life, 21 September 1978.

Preservation and Personality: York and Chester – II, John Cornforth, Country Life, 28 September 1978.

Chester: Progress in Conservation 1981 A report prepared for the Council of Europe in connection with the Fourth European Symposium of Historic Towns – Fribourg, Switzerland. Available from the Director of Technical Services, Chester City Council.

The City Conservation Programme in Chester, the award-winning submission for the 1981 European Prize for the Preservation of Historic Monuments. Available from Donald W. Insall & Associates.

Film

The Conservation Game – prepared by the DOE and the consultants in 1975 to show how the Conservation Action Programme was organised, and the results on the ground. Obtainable from the DOE Central Film Library.

Lectures

Illustrated lectures have been given to professional, educational and other bodies, in many towns at home and on overseas visits to promote and exchange experiences gained in the Chester Conservation Action Programme. Verbatim notes are available from Donald W. Insall & Associates.

Aerofilms: 26a. Leonard Baart: 62b. James Brotherhood: 60a, 60b. Chester City Council: 18a, 29b, 55a, 56c, 69a; photograph by Carol Law, 4a. Chester City Record Office and Chester Archeological Society: 17a. Cheshire County Council: 50b. Christopher Dalton for Donald W. Insall: 57c, 61b, 71b, 72c, 74a, 76d, 76e. Robin Clayton Partnership: 41b. Crown Copyright: Map No. 1, 14a, 28a, 35a, 36a, 37a, 41c, 43a, 44b, 44c, 59b, 64a, 66b, 66c, 76c, 84b, c. George Green of Chester: 86a. Donald W. Insall: 29a, 31a, 33a, 33b, 34a, 38b, 39a, 40a, 41a, 43b, 44a, 45a, 45b, 47b, 50a, 58b, 67a, 69c, 71a, 75a, 76a, 76f, 77c, 77d, 79a, 81a, 82a, 90a. Gerry Lockley: 3a. John Mills: 65a. Grosvenor Museum: 6a. National Monuments Record: 15a, 16a, 31b, 32a, 51a, 55a, 63a, 68b, 68c, 69b, 72b, 81b, 84a, 86c. N. W. Photographers: 77a, 77b. Vernon D. Shaw: 56b, 67a. Victoria and Albert Museum: 78a. Thos Ward: 46a, 47a; for Donald W. Insall: 76b.

Index

References to the text are indicated by paragraph numbers (eg 1.2, 4.12.1, etc) and references to the illustration by the page number and its position on that page (eg 10a, 46b, etc).
Abbreviations Ack's: Acknowledgements; App.: Appendix.